MW00379322

THE GREEN NEW DEAL VS. THE NEW SILK ROAD

The Deep State Drives for De-population as the World Grasps for a Real Future

By

Matthew J.L. Ehret

The Green New Deal vs. The New Silk Road

Canadian Patriot- Green New Deal vs the New Silk Road © 2019 by Matthew J.L. Ehret. All Rights Reserved.

All rights reserved. No part of this book may be reproduced in any form or by any electronic or mechanical means including information storage and retrieval systems, without permission in writing from the author. The only exception is by a reviewer, who may quote short excerpts in a review.

Cover designed by Jonathon Ludwig

Matthew J.L. Ehret
Visit my website at www.canadianpatriot.org

Printed in the United States of America

First Printing: April 2019
Canadian Patriot Press

ISBN: 9781091088092

CONTENTS

LETTER OF TRANSMITTAL

A disturbing reality has begun to dawn upon an ever greater spectrum of the world's population in recent years. This disturbing reality has much to do with the fact that the denial which has held world markets precariously in place since the 2008 housing bubble crash is no longer sustainable. Whether one may wish that this post-1971 Trans-Atlantic economy continue on indefinitely into the future, or not, the fact remains that hopes and desires have little to do with the fact that this particular banking system will crash. The question now remains: What will replace it?

Two opposing worldviews have come to present themselves onto the world stage in recent years. One seeks to revive the outlook of America's best traditions expressed in the form of great infrastructure projects and win-win cooperation and the other is committed to a return to an outdated system of governance premised upon "hereditary power of a ruling elite" and global governance under a divided world at conflict with itself.

Where the system governed by a technocratic elite centered in London demands a Green New Deal in order to combat "climate change" (although really promoting depopulation), the powers of Eurasia, led especially by China and Russia demand a genuine New Deal in the form of the Belt and Road Initiative, banking reform and long term investments into science and infrastructure. This Eurasian driven process has increasingly awakened the forgotten spirit of nation building among western governments which have witnessed a return to nationalist movements taking power in Europe and the Americas. The return to nationalism has taken the form of the Italian government which has announced its intention to become the first G7 nation to officially join the Belt and Road Initiative and even the United States whose current president has conducted a two year long battle with the British-directed Deep State.

The fact that the Green agenda is being put to the test for the first time under President Trump's Committee on Climate Security is a breath of fresh air for anyone who wants a future that permits for Earth's population to finally arise from poverty and lack of development.

This issue of the Canadian Patriot is devoted not only to shedding light on Canada's role within this unfolding struggle between systems, but we sincerely desire that Canada take this crisis as an opportunity to re-awaken a forgotten spirit of true nation building which once drove our leap into the modern age in the decades after WWII.

SNC LAVALIN AND THE CANADIAN YELLOW VESTS UNDER ATTACK

The Physical Economy is Melting Down and a Fight for a New System is on

While hundreds of yellow vest-sporting truck drivers hailing from Alberta arrived in Ottawa this week to protest the barricades imposed on the oil sector by the current Liberal Government, a storm of controversy simultaneously struck resulting in the resignation of a cabinet member as well as Trudeau's principal advisor over a scandal tied to Montreal-based construction giant SNC-Lavalin and throwing the government into a crisis.

On first glance one may make the popular error of assuming this to be a "perfect storm of divine justice" hitting a beleaguered government whose corrupt acts have gone too long unpunished. Reality, however is rarely quite so simple.

The fact is that the attack on SNC Lavalin and the attack on those blue collar workers of Canada who are watching

their means of livelihood systematically destroyed by carbon taxes, and the cancellation of infrastructure projects such as the trans mountain pipeline have at their origins, the same dirty hand. This dirty hand has a British pedigree and is sometimes called the Deep State and it is useful to keep in mind that it is this Deep State that seeks to reduce the global population to "ecologically sustainable levels" and overthrow the Westphalian system of sovereign nation state. These acts are only possible to the degree that a global paradigm of zero technological growth were to be maintained, and today, this policy is masquerading Delphically as a "Green New Deal".

For those who may not be aware, the SNC Lavalin scandal centers around the apparent pressure which the Prime Minister's Office put upon Justice Minister Wilson-Raybould who, as the story was published in a February 7, 2019 Globe and Mail article days before her resignation, was expected to intervene upon a Quebec court corruption case that threatens to annihilate the existence of SNC Lavalin as a player in Canadian infrastructure development. The "heroic" Raybould took a stand and resigned in protest and while it is not necessary to speculate about the exact mechanisms operating behind the scenes, but something much larger is at play.

As it stands now, if found guilty the construction giant which is an international force in infrastructure and nuclear projects, would face a 10 year ban on federal contracts.

Canadian PM Justin Trudeau and his lead handler Gerald Butts (former President of the World Wildlife Fund of Canada and Bilderberg participant) who resigned seconds after Raybould.

Canadian PM Justin Trudeau and his lead handler Gerald Butts (former President of the World Wildlife Fund of Canada and Bilderberg participant) who resigned seconds after Raybould.

While the court case nominally centers on the issue of bribes that SNC undertook in the construction of a major super hospital in 2012, the truth runs much deeper and touches upon a battle between two opposing systems which are now clashing globally. These systems are defined by two incompatible paradigms- one based upon an open system of multipolar (ie: pro-nation state) dynamics centered on win-win cooperation and unbounded technological progress. The other is a closed system shaped by a commitment to a unipolar, technocratically-governed mechanics shaped by zero-sum thinking. You can guess which vision is dominant in the Canadian federal government which features a Prime Minister who bragged in 2015 that "Canada is the world's first post-national state."

China and Russia's Open System

Today, Russia and China represent a unified force for development under the unified dynamic of the Belt and Road Initiative which has unleashed a program of productive credit generation tied not to speculation of fictitious assets as is the case in Wall Street, but rather great infrastructure and science both in Eurasia and abroad.

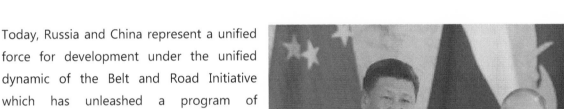

While the technocratic/Deep State agenda has always been committed to global government and depopulation, the Russia-China program is vectored around an openness to work even with those countries which have acted as enemies. Putin's February 20, 2019 state of the nation speech laid out those terms clearly when he said: "We are not interested in confrontation and we do not want it, especially with a global power like the United States of America. However, it seems that our partners fail to notice the depth and pace of change around the world and where it is headed."

This echoes the sentiments of Chinese President Xi Jinping, who stated in 2017: "We should foster a new type of international relations featuring win-win cooperation; and we should forge partnerships of dialogue with no confrontation and of friendship rather than alliance. All countries should respect each other's sovereignty, dignity and

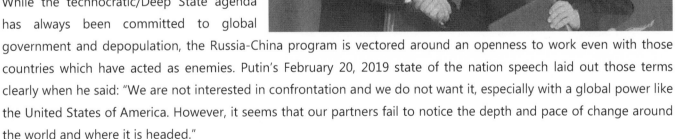

territorial integrity, each other's development paths and social systems, and each other's core interests and major concerns."

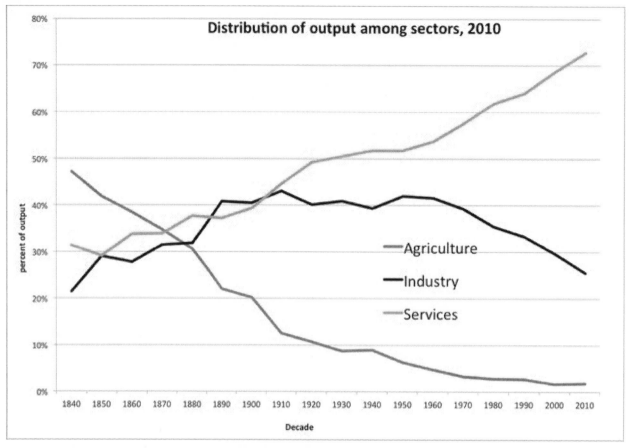

Over fifty years of post-industrialism and consumerism have unleashed a process that has rendered the nations of the west largely impotent and incapable of producing enough to sustain local populations, nor even maintain (let alone improve) its own crumbling infrastructure base. A sad shadow of once great construction capabilities still exists in various forms and to the degree that such capabilities are not directed to "green/zero growth" infrastructure, it is believed in certain technocratic corners those firms must be punished. These technocrats exemplify a religious-like commitment to a New World Order is no longer relevant in the new world system of cooperation now emerging.

SNC Lavalin Resists the Deep State Attack on National Sovereignty

If the western nations were to accept the new paradigm offered by Putin and Xi Jinping, then the deployment of those productive forces exemplified by SNC Lavalin, Bombardier, Aecon Ltd, etc... would be vital both in the construction of great projects abroad and at home alike. It is no co-incidence that such companies have been under attack by the Deep State, especially since the 2011 regime change war on Libya that destroyed much of the SNC-built infrastructure plan known as the Great Manmade River. In fact, after a quick evaluation of the major international projects which SNC Lavalin has committed to since that 2011 travesty, it should come as no surprise that this company has distinguished itself as a cooperative partner with both China and Russia on Belt and Road Projects, nuclear power generation, oil and mineral development and transportation infrastructure both in Russia and China's borders and beyond.

In June 2011 SNC Lavalin, which operates in over 100 countries, adopted a new international strategy by purchasing Atomic Energy Canada Ltd for $15 million from the Federal government, taking over control of Canada's nuclear science and engineering sector. This purchase created an unexpected potential for international nuclear cooperation outside the control of the Privy Council-run Deep State in Ottawa, as the seed became free to select the soil of another garden.

It became apparent where this more fertile soil was located in 2012 which began with an initiative to tighten cooperation with Russia through the acquisition of 48% ownership of the Russian mineral/oil giant Vnipineft and then 49% co-ownership of a joint venture company alongside the Russian Development Bank in 2013 which placed SNC Lavalin in a position to provide technical and financial oversight and support for all infrastructure projects undertaken by the Russian Development Bank.

After establishing firm points of Russian cooperation in an environment increasingly defined by an anti-Russian ABM missile shield and asymmetrical warfare in Ukraine and Syria, SNC Lavalin then began a program of vigorous cooperation with China's Belt and Road Initiative beginning in earnest in July 2014 with a Memorandum of Understanding (MOU) between SNC and the China National Nuclear Corporation (CNNC) in Vancouver Canada. SNC CEO Preston Swafford then stated "we are pleased to sign this strategic partnership agreement with CNNC to develop nuclear and uranium projects in China, while pursuing high-potential opportunities abroad. These projects have the potential to generate billions of dollars for the Canadian and Chinese economies, while supporting China's growing demand for energy"

In September 2016, an agreement was reached between SNC Lavalin, CNNC and the Shanghai Electrical Group Company Ltd to "develop, market and build the Advanced Fuel CANDU reactor" which will essential close the fuel cycle rendering buried deposits of depleted and recycled uranium a valuable source of fuel. On August 7, 2018 another agreement was reached between SNC and the Third Qinshan Nuclear Power Company to implement an advanced 37M fuel for all CANDU Reactors in Qinshan.

Ever afraid of more cooperation between Canadian construction firms and China, the Federal deep state intervened at the final stages of a long-planned deal in May 2018 wherein China's Construction Civil Engineering Ltd was supposed to purchase Canada's nearly defunct Aecon Ltd. Construction giant, destroying yet another opportunity for Canadian interests to be integrated into Belt and Road projects both in Eurasia and even in North America.

Today, several leading SNC Lavalin executives who were responsible for those above mentioned development strategies are either facing severe jail time or are sitting in prison for charges of bribery and while Aecon rots without international (or national contracts of merit), SNC Lavalin faces the real danger of a Canadian shutdown leaving China, Russia and other countries seeking a future very little to work with when dealing with Canada.

The Left vs Right Myth Crumbles

The Alberta blue collar protesters desperate for a physical productive economy are demanding a government policy which puts people and the nation before technocratic ideology (green or monetarist alike). The industrial sector which produces infrastructure, science and technology are desperate for an environment in which to thrive and which permits for long term planning and growth which nation states are uniquely positioned to provide. The simplistic narrative that SNC Lavalin is just another big bad corporation that manipulated a corrupt government at the expense of the common man as is being now promoted in the media is full of holes and should be seriously questioned.

Rather than buy into such stories that rely on class struggles of rich vs poor, it would be better to recognize that the only true conflict within human history is defined by paradigms that are committed to progress and improvement vs stagnation and enslavement. Class struggles and self-regulating mystical market places have never existed as a causal force for anything terrible important.

As China and Russia are now ushering in a new system which a sitting American President has expressed open willingness to cooperate with, this oligarchy is petrified that the "left vs right" narratives it has spun so carefully and for so long are crumbling leaving only the truth. The time has come for nation state republics defending the general welfare of their own and neighboring populations

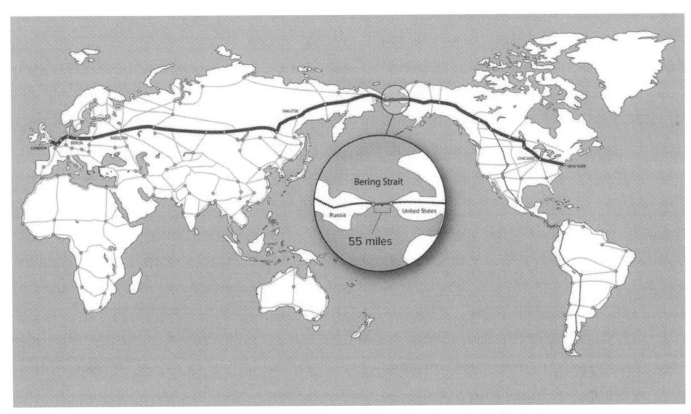

A quick overview of the current Belt and Road Initiative. Image from the Schiller Institute

CANADA'S SPACE GAMBIT AND THE UN-RAVELLING OF THE EMPIRE'S GREAT GAME

On February 28, 2019 a new policy announcement was made in Ottawa Canada that called for a re-orientation towards space exploration in partnership with NASA on an endeavor known as the Lunar Orbital Platform-Gateway (LOP-G) program.

This program was first announced at a Press conference in the morning with Canadian Prime Minister Justin Trudeau accompanied by several fellow MPs and two young astronauts. The press conference also featured an inspired presentation by David St. Jacques, the French Canadian astronaut now working alongside American and Russian counterparts on the International Space Station who discussed the ultimate purpose of mankind as a species destined to explore deep space and therein discover our common identity. St Jacques stated:

"The International Space Station... is an example of what humanity can accomplish when we go beyond our differences and work together in peace for the benefit of all... I trained for years with people from around the world and what I realized is that the place we come from isn't as important as the goal that brings us together- exploration and the advance of knowledge... Here on ISS we have been learning and gaining experience. Now building on what we learned we are getting ready to take the next step. Gateway will be an outpost where humans can live in lunar orbit, where we will learn to live even more autonomously from mother earth."

The essentials of the program involve a pledge to spend $2 billion over 24 years towards the Lunar Gateway and while it will focus upon Canada's specialization in Robotics, will have a much more wide ranging set of goals including service as a Science laboratory, a test site for new technologies, a meeting location for the exploration to the surface of the moon, mission control center for lunar operations and a future stepping stone for voyages to Mars.

Responding to the Press Conference, NASA Administrator Jim Bridenstine enthusiastically wrote:

"NASA is thrilled that Canada is the first international partner for the Gateway lunar outpost. Space exploration is in Canada's DNA. In 1962, Canada became the third nation to launch a satellite into orbit with Alouette 1. Today, Canada leads the world in space-based robotic capabilities, enabling critical repairs to the Hubble Space Telescope and construction of the International Space Station. Our new collaboration on Gateway will enable our broader international partnership to get to the Moon and eventually to Mars"

This surprising shift towards a pro-NASA space program reflects a deeper pro-China maneuver underway within the Trump Administration which has occurred in spite of years of severe resistance from the Deep State.

It is no secret that NASA's Gateway program was itself made possible by the advanced vision which both Russia and China have expressed towards a long term deep space orientation; with Russia having already announced a permanent lunar colony by 2040 (with construction slated to begin in 2025), and China's multi-phase Chang'e program which has just made a milestone landing on the far side of the Moon. The fact that the January 3, 2019 Chang'e 4 landing occurred with collaboration with NASA was no small feat and represented a gigantic success in overthrowing the 2011 ban on US-China cooperation on space imposed by the Obama administration.

Opposing Reason: A Manufactured Scandal

Ironically, of the eight questions posed by the press after the main presentations had been given, not a single one addressed the issue of space. Instead, the Prime Minister received the "Donald Trump treatment" through a barrage of questions relating to the SNC Lavalin scandal now unfolding, and the scathing testimony given by former Justice Minister Jody Wilson-Raybould the day before which currently threatens to not only force Justin Trudeau's resignation but also destroy SNC Lavalin's presence in Canada for the next 10 years.

The fact that Wilson-Raybould's resignation occurred days before Justin Trudeau's principal advisor Gerald Butts resigned, indicates that a larger fight is underway within the ranks of the Anglo-Canadian establishment.

The question remains: What is happening within Canada? Thousands of Albertan protesters have dawned yellow vests due to the potential demise of the Trans Mountain Pipeline- several hundred of whom have made national headlines by driving a convoy of trucks across the continent to Ottawa last week in order to protest a government which has failed to defend Canadian jobs and development. Many of these protesters are even celebrating the SNC scandal which now threatens to topple the government. But is this scandal truly what it appears?

To answer any of these questions responsibly means taking a higher top-down assessment of the situation with the unconventional idea that perhaps not everything in politics is reducible to monetary profit and that Canada's often paradoxical behavior may only be understood by observing a higher global operating system FIRST and then evaluating a purposeful role which Canada plays within such a larger "great game".

Canada's Role in Advancing a Green New Deal

With the formation of the Canada 2020 think tank after the defeat of the Liberal government of Paul Martin in 2006, a new "green technocratic" policy was created in order to counteract the threat to the New Liberal World Order posed by an ascendant China which was beginning to unify ever more with Russia. With the 2012 imposition of Justin Trudeau as an Obama-modelled figurehead leader of the Liberal Party, this program was put into motion in order to undermine China's long term growth orientation through the creation of a "Canada-China Special Relationship". In 2014, none other than Obama's former Treasury Secretary Larry Summers outlined this strategy in Ottawa as he keynoted the Canada

Larry Summer's bizarre appearance in Canada's upper echelons is causing many to ask: what is really controlling Canada?

2020 conference alongside his close friend Chrystia Freeland (now Canadian Foreign Minister and possible candidate to replace Trudeau). During that 2014 presentation Summers and Freeland advocated a new system based upon a "Green New Deal" to replace the current bankrupt order.

Franklin Roosevelt in 1933

For those who may be unfamiliar, the term "New Deal" refers to the system ushered in by President Franklin Roosevelt in 1932 which involved vast state intervention into a financial system driven into four years of depression due to rampant de-regulation, and Wall Street speculation. The New Deal itself was driven by government regulation of the banks and long term credit invested into major infrastructure projects which allowed America to slowly recover from the decay of depression. The green version of the New Deal advocated by the likes of Summers, Freeland and other Malthusians today is a twisted perversion of the original since it is entirely based upon investments into "sustainable" energy infrastructure (windmills, biomass and solar panels). Rather than INCREASING the productive powers of a nation as the original accomplished during the 1930s, the 21st century green doppelganger can do nothing but contract a nation's productivity and capacity to support its population.

To advance this agenda, Canada had to win China's trust on the one hand by demonstrating that various "goods and services" could be offered to the rising dragon, while positioning itself to induce China to adopt "Green New Deal" reforms on the other. If accomplished successfully, this plan would sabotage the potential formation of a grouping of Eurasian-led nations powerful enough to challenge the Financier oligarchy.

What were those assets that Canada brought to the potential deal?

1- A Cheap Resources Honey Pot. Canada does, after all, hold the world's greatest untapped reservoirs of oil and natural gas, as well as a multitude of other strategic raw materials.

2- Nuclear science capabilities exemplified in AECL and the unique CANDU system owned by SNC Lavalin since 2011

3- Infrastructure building capabilities exemplified by such giants as Bombardier, SNC Lavalin, and Aecon Inc. which could be deployed in the assistance of Belt and Road projects globally.

Beginning with the election of Trump and continuing with China's official rejection of Canada's special relationship in 2017, it started to become obvious that the Trudeau card was significantly less valuable than it was previously hoped. As 2018 unfolded, all three Canadian capabilities mentioned above started falling apart as we will briefly review below.

1- Tipping over the honey pot:

Efforts to open the Asian markets to Canadian oil and natural gas were entirely hinged on the construction of the Trans Mountain pipeline and a 5 year fight to build it began. Just three months after the Federal Government jumped in with $4.5 billion to buy the floundering project, the Federal Court of Appeals stepped in and blocked the construction on August 20, 2018. No significant channel currently exists to export gas to China as 99.2% of Canada's oil goes to the USA. Observing the unreliable basket case behavior, China (a country which thinks hundreds of years ahead and requires stability) ultimately threw their destiny into their "special relationship" with Russia, pushing ahead with the $55 billion "Power of Siberia" pipeline to China which is now 99% finished and will soon supply over 25% of China's energy needs.

2- Nuclear Cooperation strangled with the take down of SNC Lavalin

With a commitment to end poverty, pollution, and drive the vast Belt and Road Initiative, China has become the world's biggest developer of nuclear power, having grown from 3 to 38 reactors in a mere 20 years, with an additional 18 under active construction. SNC Lavalin's ownership of Atomic Energy of Canada Ltd. (AECL) brought it into the unique position of handling Canada's CANDU nuclear reactor system which China has a major vested interest in. Several major treaties were signed between China and SNC Lavalin between 2014-2018 in order to integrate nuclear cooperation- one of the most important being a project to close the fuel cycle using Advanced 37M fuel.

3- The Sabotage of Canada's Involvement with the Belt and Road

When China attempted to purchase the near-defunct yet highly valuable Canadian construction giant Aecon in May 2018, the Deep State intervened when it became evident that such a purchase could not be permitted if China were the force making the rules rather than western technocrats. This intervention came as a surprise to some who recalled that Canada had formerly done everything possible to attract China's investments into Canadian enterprises. It was only in 2012, that the Harper government, seeking to move in more closely to China, passed the Omnibus Bill C-38 undoing in one stroke decades of environmental protection, making vast tracts of otherwise inaccessible land open for resource development. This act was accompanied by the over-riding of federal legislation which forbade foreign ownership of large Canadian businesses when China's National Offshore Oil Co. (CNOOC) was given the green light to purchase Canada's Nexen gas company for $15.1 billion.

With that intervention, another opportunity for Canada's participation in the Belt and Road Initiative went up in smoke.

We have come to the moment of truth

Nothing short of a profound shift in the global operating system can have any durable positive effect upon humanity as a whole. That profound shift must take on the character of a leap from a "closed system" of entropy which is the framework under which the London-based financier oligarchy wields its power today, towards an "open system" modelled on the principle of anti-entropy. Where the former system relies on monopolising fixed resources within a zero-sum system of "diminishing rates of return", the latter system prioritises creative discoveries that increase mankind's power over nature in a manner which is in accord with the natural tendency for life to grow and thrive under states of increasing creative potential.

The Belt and Road Initiative and it's orientation towards "win-win cooperation" alongside the Russia-China program for unbounded deep space exploration and nuclear power investment have exemplified the potential for "open-system thinking" in the 21st century.

The fact that America under Donald Trump has begun to overthrow "closed system" institutions like the Trans-Pacific Partnership, NAFTA, COP21, and even the ban on US-China space cooperation represents one of the most important flanking maneuvers seen since John F. Kennedy called for US-Russia joint space cooperation to end the Cold War in 1963.

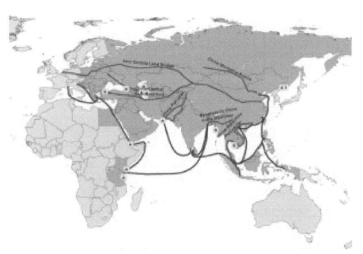

Major Eurasian corridors of the Belt and Road Initiative

The London-Wall Street led financial system which has been such a key component of the modern British Empire is obviously bankrupt and over-ripe for a collapse. Had the China-Russia alliance not grown to such empowered proportions, surely such a collapse would be a desirable outcome for those Malthusian technocrats loyal to the oligarchy. Surely a controlled collapse would not be a terrible thing for anyone who wished to establish a new "operating system" based upon a post-nation state order of green depopulation (today advanced by advocates of the Green New Deal where the "values" of money are to be determined by increasing rates of decreases of humanity's "carbon footprints"). But that was not to be.

Not only have Russia and China successfully resisted the post-Libyan regime change order by blocking the many attempts to overthrow the Syrian government, but new alternative financial mechanisms have been created to issue productive credit not for speculation, but for long term development both in Eurasia as well as Africa and Latin America.

Russia-gate has increasingly failed to overthrow the presidency of Donald Trump with no evidence ever found to substantiate Deep State Mueller's claims of "Russian collusion". Together, Russia and China have created a political-economic block that includes the Shanghai Cooperation Organisation, BRICS and many more institutions which not only defend the principle of sovereignty, but the right of true development of those productive powers of labour that can only be driven by the ever increasing powers of human cognition. This system is open, unbounded, increasingly nuclear-powered, space-based and vectored upon an infinite potential for growth.

When all is said and done, we see an over-bloated empire, drunk through overconsumption of belief in its own arrogant infallibility and self-destructing under its own internal contradictions.

Having committed itself to an ideologically extreme position of zero compromise when faced with the creation of a new operating system that will not tolerate its existence, the oligarchy's behavior indicates that it prefers to "rule in hell than serve in heaven", to the point that it would even risk destroying its own basis for existence.

Whether a policy of a Green New Deal is advanced by the Deep State, or whether a true New Deal centering on Glass-Steagall bank reform, productive credit emitted through national banks and great projects of science, high speed rail, energy and space exploration remain the questions that must yet be answered.

WHY HAS THE WEST DESTROYED ITS OWN INDUSTRIAL BASE?

The Case of Maurice Strong Re-visited

With the arrival of convoys of Albertan yellow vest protesters in Ottawa demanding an end to the zero-growth ideology dominating the Federal policy landscape and manifesting itself in the "Green New Deal" being advanced across Europe and North America, it is fair to inquire why Canada and other nations of the Trans-Atlantic abandoned a policy of industrial growth and progress that had once caused the greatest rates increase of living standards and population potential in human history. This trend towards de-industrialization not only destroyed the once full spectrum national economies of the west but also crippled key industrial sectors which are so vital for national infrastructure creation. The current attacks on SNC Lavalin and the advanced energy sector are no exceptions to this trend.

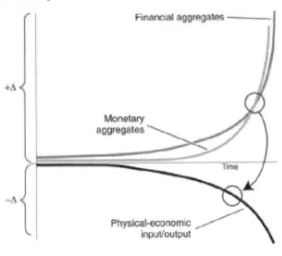

The Collapse Reaches a Critical Point of Instability

Since the 1971 floating of the US dollar on the global markets, and the 1973 creation of the Petro dollar, the world has experienced a consistent collapse of productive manufacturing jobs, infrastructure investment, a long-term planning on the one hand and a simultaneous increase of de-regulation, short term speculation, and low-wage retail jobs on the other. During this post 1971 process of decline, debt slavery became a norm both in developed countries and developing sector nations alike, while outsourcing caused the castration of national sovereignty and an ever greater reliance on "cheap labor" and "cheap resources" from abroad. The most concrete model of this collapse was unveiled to the world in 1996 by the late American statesman and economist Lyndon LaRouche, in what is known as the Triple Curve Collapse Function.

Some have called this collapse "a failure of globalization". Executive Intelligence Review's Latin American Desk Editor Dennis Small has repeatedly stated over many years that this characterization is false. Globalization should rather be seen as a complete success– in that when it is viewed from a top-down perspective, it becomes increasingly clear that the architects of this policy achieved exactly what they set out to do. That intention was to impose an artificial closed/zero-sum game paradigm upon a species whose distinguishing characteristic is its creative reason and the capacity for constant perfectibility both on the earth and ever more so beyond.

Introducing Maurice Strong

A primary figure in the oligarchy's tool box of sociopathic agents who shaped this program for zero sum thinking over the years is a Canadian-born operative by the name of Maurice Strong. Despite having died in 2015, Strong's life and legacy are worth revisiting as they provide the modern reader a powerful, albeit ugly insight into the methods and actions of the British-Deep State agenda that so mis-shaped world history through the latter half of the 20th century.

Having dealt in previous articles with Strong's role as a recruit of Rockefeller assets in the 1950s, an oil baron, vice president of Power Corporation by 30, Liberal Party controller, Privy Councilor, and founder of Canada's neo-colonial external aid policy towards Africa, we will focus here on the role Strong has played since 1968 in subverting the anti-entropic potential of Canada and the world at large. It was through this post-1968 role that Strong performed his most valued work for the genocidal agenda of his British masters who seek to reduce the world population to a "carrying capacity" of less than a billion.

RIO and Global Governance

In 1992, Maurice Strong had been assigned to head the second Earth Summit (the first having been the 1972 Stockholm Conference on the Human Environment also chaired by Strong). The Rio Summit had established a new era in the consolidation of NGOs and corporations under the genocidal green agenda of controlled starvation masquerading behind the dogma of "sustainability'. This doctrine was formalized with Agenda 21 and the Earth Charter, co-authored by Mikhail Gorbachev, Jim MacNeill and Strong during the 1990s. At the opening of the Rio Summit, Strong announced that industrialized countries had "developed and benefited from the unsustainable patterns of production and consumption which have produced our present dilemma. It is clear that current lifestyles and consumption patterns of the affluent middle class, involving high meat intake, consumption of large amounts of frozen and convenience foods, use of fossil fuels, appliances, home and work-place air-conditioning, and suburban housing- are not sustainable. A shift is necessary toward lifestyles less geared to environmentally damaging consumption patterns."

In a 1992 essay entitled ***From Stockholm to Rio: A Journey Down a Generation***, published by the UN Conference on Environment and Development, Strong wrote:

"The concept of national sovereignty has been an immutable, indeed sacred, principle of international relations. It is a principle which will yield only slowly and reluctantly to the new imperatives of global environmental cooperation. What is needed is recognition of the reality that in so many fields, and this is particularly true of environmental issues, it is simply not feasible for sovereignty to be exercised unilaterally by individual nation-states, however powerful. The global community must be assured of environmental security."

Two years earlier, Strong gave an interview[1] wherein he described a "fiction book" he was fantasizing about writing which he described in the following manner:

"What if a small group of world leaders were to conclude that the principal risk to the Earth comes from the actions of the rich countries? And if the world is to survive, those rich countries would have to sign an agreement reducing their impact on the environment. Will they do it? The group's conclusion is 'no'. The rich countries won't do it. They won't change. So, in order to save the planet, the group decides: Isn't the only hope for the planet that the industrialized civilizations collapse? Isn't it our responsibility to bring that about?"

When this statement is held up parallel to this man's peculiar life, we quickly come to see that the barrier between reality and fiction is more than a little blurry.

The Destruction of Nuclear Power

It is vital to examine Strong's role in crippling Canada's potential to make use of nuclear power, one of the greatest beacons of hope mankind has ever had to break out of the current "fixed" boundaries to humanity's development. Indeed, the controlled use of the atom, along with the necessary discovery of new universal principles associated with this endeavor, have always represented one of the greatest strategic threats to the oligarchic system, which depends on a closed system of fixed resources in order to both manage current populations and justify global governance under "objective" frameworks of logic. Fission and fusion processes exist on a level far beyond those fixed parameters that assume the earth's "carrying capacity" is no greater than the 2 billion souls envisioned by today's London-centered oligarchy. If mankind were to recognize his unique creative potential to continuously transcend his limitations by discovering and creating new resources, no empire could long exist. With Canada as the second nation

---

[1] "The Wizard Of the Baca Grande," WEST magazine of Alberta, Canada, May 1990

to have civilian nuclear power, and a frontier science culture in physics and chemistry, the need to destroy this potential in the mind of the British Deep State of Canada was great indeed.

To get a better sense of the anti-nuclear role Strong has played in Canadian science policy, we must actually go back once again to Strong's reign at the Department of External Aid in 1966.

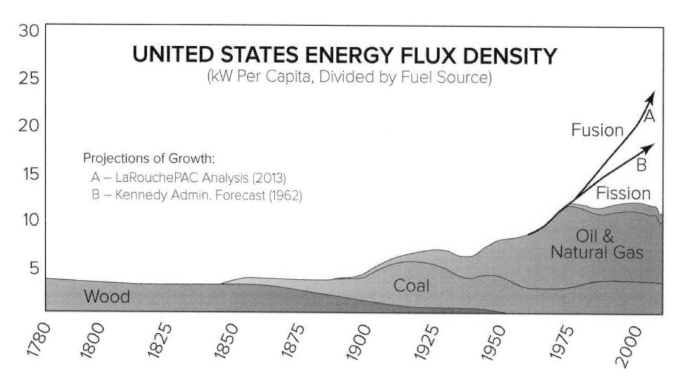

Humanity's trend towards utilizing ever more dense forms of fire was always driven by a commitment to scientific and technological progress. The realization that this process drives the increase of human potential population density (both in quantity and quality of life) was recognized at the turn of the 20th century and serves as the foundation for American economist Lyndon LaRouche's method of economic forecasting. The graph above features American per capita access to energy and the post-1975 sabotage of the expected transition to nuclear fission and fusion

Technological Apartheid for Africa

A key reason that Strong had been brought into Canada's Civil Service to head up the External Aid office in 1966 was to sabotage the international efforts leading scientists and statesmen had achieved in making Canada an exporter of its original CANDU reactors. Since 1955, leading patriots within Atomic Energy Canada Ltd. (AECL) and the National Research Council such as C.D. Howe and his collaborator C.W. Mackenzie, ensured that the export of advanced nuclear technology was made available to developing countries such as India and Pakistan. In Canada this policy was advanced vigorously by Prime Minister John Diefenbaker, who also saw atomic power as the key to world peace.

The banners under which this advanced technology transfer occurred were both the Columbo Plan and President Dwight Eisenhower's Atoms for Peace. This progressive approach to international development defined "external aid" not around IMF conditionalities, or simply money for its own sake, but rather as the transfer of the most advanced science and technology to poor countries with the explicit intention that all nations would attain true sovereignty. This is the model that China has adopted today under the Belt and Road Initiative.

When Strong got to work in External Aid, and later formed the Canadian International Development Agency, Canada's relationship to "LDCs" (lesser developed countries) became reduced to advancing "appropriate technologies" under the framework of monetarism and a perverse form of systems analysis. After JFK's assassination, a parallel operation was conducted in America's USAid. No technology or advanced infrastructure policy necessary for the independence of former colonies were permitted under this precursor to what later became known as "sustainability" and "zero growth". Under Strong's influence, Canada's role became perverted into inducing LDCs to become obedient to IMF/World Bank "conditionalities" and the reforms of their bureaucracies demanded by the OECD in order to receive money. Both in Canada and in developing countries, Strong was among the key agents who oversaw the implementation of the OECD's strategy of "closed systems analysis" for national policy management.

Petrol and Pandas

In his role as President of Petro Canada (1976-78), Strong endorsed the national call to create a nuclear moratorium for Canada which had been carried out by the Canadian Coalition for Nuclear Responsibility in 1977. This document not only demanded an immediate halt to the continuation of all reactors then under construction, but also made the sophistical argument that more jobs could be created if "ecologically friendly" energy sources and conservation methods were developed instead of nuclear and fossil fuels. Strange desires coming from an oil executive, but not so strange considering Strong's 1978-1981 role as Vice-President of the World Wildlife Fund (WWF), an organization founded by the British and Dutch monarchies as a Royal Dutch Shell initiative in 1963. Strong was Vice President during the same interval that WWF co-founder Prince Philip was its President.

Bloomfield, Black and Munk, alongside Strong are three of the most prolific of the Canadian founding members Prince Bernhard and Prince Philip's 1001 Club

In 1971, while still heading up the External Aid Department, Strong was a founding member of the 1001 Club, which was an elite international organization created by Prince Bernhard of the Netherlands created to finance the emerging green agenda for world governance. The 1001 Club worked in tandem with Prince Bernhard's other secretive club known as the "Bilderberg Group" which he founded in 1954. In this position, Strong helped to recruit 80 Canadian "initiates" to this elite society otherwise known as "Strong's Kindergarten", the most prominent being Lord Conrad Black, Barrick Gold's Peter Munk (1927-2018) and Permindex's late Sir Louis Mortimer Bloomfield (1906-1984). As documented elsewhere, the latter was discovered to be at the heart of the plot to assassinate President John F. Kennedy by New Orleans District Attorney Jim Garrison.

Strong Decapitates Ontario Nuclear Energy

By 1992, Strong had completed his role heading the Rio Earth Summit in Brazil and had returned to his native land to attempt to finalize the dismantling of Canada's nuclear program in his new assignment as President of Ontario Hydro, a position he held from 1992 to 1995 under the formal invitation of Bob Rae, then-NDP Premier of Ontario and brother of Power Corp.'s John Rae. Bob Rae later served as the leader of the Liberal Party from 2011-2013 in preparation for Justin Trudeau's appointment to become the party's new figurehead in April of 2013.

Strong was brought in to this position at the time that Ontario had the most ambitious nuclear program in North America and was proving to be a thorn in the side of the zero-growth agenda demanded by the British Empire. The completion of the massive Darlington system in Ontario had demonstrated what successful long-term science planning could accomplish, although the utility found itself running far over budget. The budgetary problems (which occurred during a deep recession in 1992) were used by Strong to "restructure" the provincial energy utility.

The "remedies" chosen by Strong to solve Ontario Hydro's financial woes involved immediately canceling all new planned nuclear energy development, firing 8 of the 14 directors, and downsizing the utility by laying off 14 000 employees, many of whom were the most specialized and experienced nuclear technicians in Canada.

Before leaving his post in 1995 with the fall of Bob Rae's government, Strong ensured that his work would continue with his replacement Jim MacNeill who headed Ontario Hydro from 1994 to 1997. MacNeill was co-architect of both the Earth Charter and the genocidal Agenda 21 during the Rio Summit and a long time Deep State agent. Under MacNeill, Strong's mandate to unnecessarily shut down eight reactors for refurbishment and one permanently was effected in 1997, while Ontario Hydro itself was broken up into three separate entities. With the irreparable loss of specialized manpower and skills Strong and MacNeill left Ontario Hydro and AECL mortally wounded for years to come.

Surprising all observers, AECL and the Ontario utilities were able to remobilize their remaining forces to pull together the successful refurbishment of all reactors– the last of which came back online in October 2012. While Canada's moratorium on nuclear power continued, with SNC Lavalin's 2011 takeover, an approach for cooperation on international nuclear construction in partnership with China began in July 2014, much to Strong's chagrin[2].

Strong's Failed Attempt to Infiltrate China

Strong in 2010 trying to convince the Chinese government to commit suicide by imposing carbon caps to itself

For much of the 21st century, Strong's talents were put to use in an attempt to subvert the aspirations of Asian development, and of a Eurasian alliance formed around the driving economic grand design of the emerging Belt and Road Initiative. Strong was deployed to Beijing University where he acted as Honorary Professor and Chairman of its Environmental Foundation and Chairman of the Advisory Board of the Institute for Research on Security and Sustainability for Northwest Asia.

In the face of the meltdown of the Trans-Atlantic economy, the Chinese have successfully resisted the Green New Deal agenda that demanded the submission of their national sovereignty to the "New World Order" of zero-growth and depopulation. In spite of this pressure, a powerful tradition of Confucianism and its commitment to progress has demonstrated its powerful influence in the various branches of the Chinese establishment who see China's only hope for survival located in its strategic partnership with Russia and long term mega projects to lift its people out of poverty and into the 22nd Century. This was made fully clear when China rejected the "special relationship" with Canada in December 2017.

---

[2] Even more surprising is that the key argument which the 1977 moratorium used to justify the cancellation of Canada's nuclear builds was that nuclear waste was impossible to manage by any other means other than million year burial while the plutonium-238 by-product created by nuclear power could be used for weapons. With the SNC-Lavalin/China agreements a strategy for implementation of both the closing of the fuel cycle using recycled and reused fuel was unleashed on the one hand while the CANDU designs were now enabling the use of the more plentiful Thorium as an alternative to Uranium which creates no plutonium and thus no threat of weapons use.

Speaking of the importance of the Belt and Road Initiative which had combined with the Eurasian Economic Union and BRICS, President Xi Jinping stated in 2017: *"We should foster a new type of international relations featuring win-win cooperation; and we should forge partnerships of dialogue with no confrontation and of friendship rather than alliance. All countries should respect each other's sovereignty, dignity and territorial integrity, each other's development paths and social systems, and each other's core interests and major concerns... In pursuing the Belt and Road Initiative, we will not resort to outdated geopolitical maneuvering. What we hope to achieve is a new model of win-win cooperation. We have no intention to form a small group detrimental to stability, what we hope to create is a big family of harmonious co-existence."*

The Belt and Road Initiative has arisen as a true opposition to the bipolar insanity of western right wing militarism/monetarism on the one side and left wing depopulation under "Green New Deals" on the other. Trillions of dollars of credit in great infrastructure projects across Eurasia, Africa and Latin America have resulted in the greatest burst of cultural optimism, productivity and if the population and leadership of the west act with the proper passion and wisdom, there is a very good opportunity to rid humanity of the legacy of Maurice Strong.

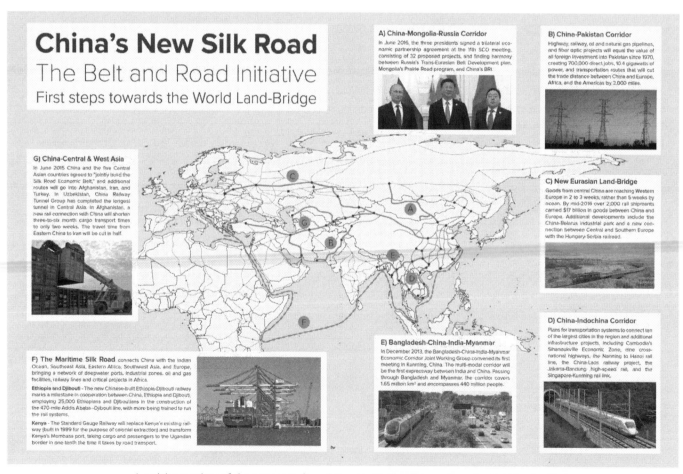

A quick overview of the current Belt and Road Initiative. Image from the Schiller Institute

CANADA'S ROLE IN BRITAIN'S ARCTIC GREAT GAME CHALLENGED BY RUSSIA AND CHINA

Since Russia's Arctic economic and military activities have grown exponentially over the past few years, western press, especially in Canada which has long shared disputed Arctic Territory with Russia, have periodically sounded warning alarms to provoke fear that the Great bear is awakening with ambitions that threaten Canada and the Free world (which are often spun as synonymous concepts).

A series of reports published across the Canadian press on have signaled that Canada must respond to Russia's aggressive posture post haste. Military think tanks have sprung up in this echo chamber in a unified call for a new Arctic strategy to counteract this "dangerous force".

Many who look upon the global strategic situation may be quick to dismiss Canada's importance in the ongoing Great Game being played by the Trans National Deep State which seeks to prevent all cooperation between Donald Trump's America and the Eurasian Alliance led by Russia and China. Canada's military is negligible some say, and it is merely a "middle power". What damage could Canada possibly do?

It is to the person asking this question that this report was written.

The British Great Game Past and Present

The first factor which such a person must recognize is the nature of the British Empire as an efficient power structure dominating the world even today. The recognition for this structure embedded through the institutions of western governments has arisen since Donald Trump's 2016 election and has been given the term "Deep State".

Under this imperial system, Canada is the second largest territory in the world with one of the lowest population densities. The British Empire has kept a tight grip on Canada over the years due to its strategic location positioned as it is between two great nations (Russia and America) who have been inclined to unite their interests in opposition to the British Empire on several focal points in history.

Find that hard to believe?

Well consider that it was the 1776 League of Armed Neutrality organized by the Russia of Catherine the Great which tipped the balance in favor of the Americans during the revolution against Great Britain, and it was Czar Alexander II's deployment of the Russian Navy to American coasts in 1863 which saved Lincoln's union from disintegration at the hands of British-steered operations of the southern confederacy. Churchill was furious that Stalin's partnership with Franklin Roosevelt favored a US-Russian alliance for post-war reconstruction. Russia and America together were instrumental in putting down the Wall Street-London funded Frankenstein monster during World War II and it was Stalin who bemoaned FDR's death by saying "the great dream is dead" as Truman ushered in the new Anglo-American Special Relationship.

The Post-WWII Order and the Rhodes Trust Origins of NATO

In the Post-WWII order, this important tendency for US-Russian partnership was directly targeted by forces loyal to the British Empire's grand strategy for global Anglo-Saxon Dominance exemplified by Sir Winston Churchill's unveiling of the Cold War during his March 5, 1946 "Iron Curtain" speech in Fulton Missouri and the follow-up creation of NATO in 1949 as a military bloc which would operate independently of the UN Security Council [1].

An under-appreciated role in the formation of NATO and international dis-order more generally during these Cold War years is the British Deep State of Canada and due to the neglect of this fact, a few words should be said about this problem here and now.

Two Deep State Rhodes Scholar operatives in Canada who were at the heart of NATO's creation: Escott Reid (left) and Lester Pearson (right)

While official narratives have tried to spin NATO's origins as the effect of an agreement amongst all western powers, the fact is that British intelligence operations are the true source, with British-trained Rhodes Scholar Escott Reid laying out the thesis for a supranational military body outside of the influence of the UN Security Council as early as August 1947. It was another two years before the design would materialize as an anti-Soviet military coalition based on the binding agreement that if one member enters a conflict, then all members must so enter.

At a Round Table-directed Conference on August 13, 1947, Reid, an ardent globalist and co-founder of the Canadian branch of the London Fabian Society *"recommended that the countries of the North Atlantic band together, under the leadership of the United States, to form 'a new regional security organization' to deter Soviet expansion."* He went on to state *"In such an organization each member state could accept a binding obligation to pool the whole of its economic and military resources with those of the other members if any power should be found to have committed aggression against any one of the members."*

The name of the British Imperial game has always been "balance of power". Manipulate society as a single closed system by monopolizing resources, and then manage the diminishing rates of return by creating conflict between potential allies. This process can be seen clearly today behind the conflicts manipulated in the South China Sea between China and Philippines, the Diaoyu-Senkaku Islands between China and Japan, wars for oil in the Middle East and the new tension being created in the Arctic. The opposing, typically "American System of Political Economy" has always disobeyed this game of "balancing a fixed system" by introducing creative change.

The American System has traditionally located its point of emphasis primarily upon creating new resources, through inventions and discoveries, rather than simply looting, consuming, and distributing what already exists. This system formulated by Benjamin Franklin, Alexander Hamilton, John Quincy Adams, Abraham Lincoln and Franklin Roosevelt proved that more energy could always be produced than was consumed IF discoveries and inventions were cultivated in a creatively developing society, shaped by concrete national intentions and bold visionary goals to increase the powers of production of society. The American System is thus in conformity with the universal principle of anti-entropy, while the British

Pierre Trudeau described his foreign policy as "creating counter-weights". Here Trudeau is featured as the 1st western head of state greeting Chairman Mao.

28

System is based on the fraudulent notion of universal entropy. Since the British system implies that the world resources are limited, then the stronger will necessarily have to loot the weaker.

Throughout the Cold War, Canada's role as a "middle power" was defined most succinctly by Fabian Society asset Pierre Elliot Trudeau, who, when asked what his foreign policy was, explained simply: "to create counterweights". That is, when the "geopolitical center of gravity" moves towards "capitalist America", then Canada must move towards befriending "socialist" Russia and its allies. When the center of gravity moves towards a Russian edge within the Great Game, then do the opposite. Although the Cold War "officially" ended in 1989, the imperial Great Game never did, and Canada's role as a British chess piece continues unabated to the present.

The Strategy of the Arctic in History

Today, the northern Arctic is among the last unexplored and undeveloped frontiers on the earth. With an area over 14 million square kilometers, this area is rich in a variety of mineral and gas deposits containing approximately 90 billion barrels of oil and 1670 trillion cubic feet of natural gas. This abundance is complicated by the fact that its borders are highly undefined, overlapping eight major nations with Canada and Russia as the dominant claimants.

In recent history, American System methods were attempted in the opening up of the Arctic for mutual development

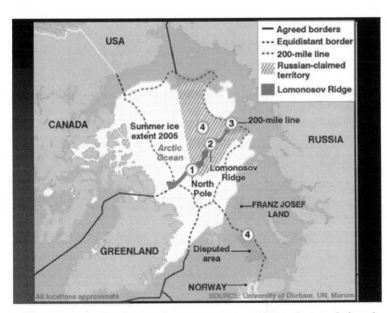

The struggle for Arctic dominance is currently being defined by the rules of British geopolitics. The above map features the layout of the arctic with doted lines defining areas still not under the control of any particular nation.

and cooperation beginning with the sale of Alaska to America in 1867 by the "American system Czar" Alexander II to the allies of Abraham Lincoln. These same forces orchestrated the construction of the Trans-Siberian railway and heavily promoted the Bering Strait Rail tunnel connecting the two great continents which arose by the turn of the century [3]. Early designs for the Russian-American rail connection were published in 1893 by Governor William Gilpin of Colorado which gained renewed support by the soon-to-be-deposed Czar Nicholas II in 1905. Russia again revived this project in 2011.

Throughout the 20th Century, Russia has developed a far greater aptitude at creating corridors of permanent habitation in the Arctic relative to their North American counterparts. Due to the Cold War dynamic of tension initiated by the British Empire after Franklin Roosevelt's death in April 1945, much that could have been accomplished, had resources not been so badly drained by Cold War militarization, was not.

The Trans Siberian Rail and the American System in Russia

After the Alaska Purchase of 1867, American System scientists and statesmen applied Lincoln's program with the help of American engineers to create the Trans-Siberian railway. Pictured top left to bottom right are Count Sergei Witte, Scientist Dimitri Mendeleev, Finance Minister Ivan A. Vyshnegradsky and the assassinated Czar Alexander II (aka: "The Great Liberator" for his freeing of the serfs).

John Diefenbaker's Northern Vision featured a vast domed Arctic City in Frobisher Bay (right)

Fig. 1:1958 Frobisher Bay Domed City design (commissioned by the Dept. of Public Works)

The beacon of light during this Cold Dark process was to be found in Canada's 13th Prime Minister John Diefenbaker, whose Northern Vision, unveiled in 1958, hinged upon his $78 million allocation for funds to construct a permanent domed nuclear powered city in Frobisher Bay (now named Iqaluit, the capital of Nunavut), as a test case for a greater nation building program in the Arctic. When Diefenbaker was run out of office in 1963 through a British-steered operation, his vision was scrapped, and a new Arctic doctrine was artificially imposed upon Canada.

This new imperial Arctic doctrine was modeled around the two (anti-nation building) measures of "conservation" of fixed ecosystems and indigenous cultures on the one side, and rapacious mineral exploitation for the increasingly deregulated "global markets" on the other. Canadian examples of this operation can be seen in the Munk School of Global Affairs, the World Wildlife Fund of Canada (whose 2nd president was the CEO of Royal Dutch Shell), and their powerful affiliate, the Walter and Duncan Gordon Foundation,

Thomas Axworthy's work for the new British Empire intersects the most influential oligarchical networks in Canada.

presided over by Pierre Trudeau's former Principal Secretary Thomas Axworthy. Barack Gold Founder and CEO Peter Munk was one of hundreds of oil barons who acted as founding members of the 1001 Club which was created by Prince Bernhardt of the Netherlands and Prince Philip of England in order to fund the WWF in its early years. Other Canadian Deep State founding members of the 1001 Club included WWF Vice Presidents Maurice Strong and Louis Mortimer Bloomfield [2].

Axworthy is a major player in the Canada 2020 machine associated with the current Liberal Party of Justin Trudeau. The overlap of major banking institutions like the Royal Bank of Canada and Scotiabank with the mineral cartels, holding companies and environmental organizations in this structure produces a very real picture that the left and the right are merely two sides of the same imperial beast.

The role of the above interests in creating the Arctic Council in 1996 (and the later Circumpolar Business Forum) was designed to trap nations into an intellectual cage of resource exploitation under free market doctrines of zero national planning on the one side, with eco-systems management and zero national planning on the other. Now that the post-1971 world financial order is on the verge of collapse, these technocrats believe that a new replacement system will allow for national planning, but only on condition that it be directed by Malthusian technocrats and aimed at the goal of lowering the population potential of the planet [5]. This agenda has come to be known as the "Green New Deal".

To re-emphasize: When observed from a top down perspective, both the "left" eco-green movement and the "right" monetarist institutions are one single thing. It is only by foolishly looking at this process from the "bottom up" that apparent differences are perceived. This is just an illusion for the credulous victims of an imperial education system who have been taught to believe their sense perceptions more than their powers of reason. The reality is that this is nothing more than British Malthusian geopolitics.

Breaking Out of the Great Game

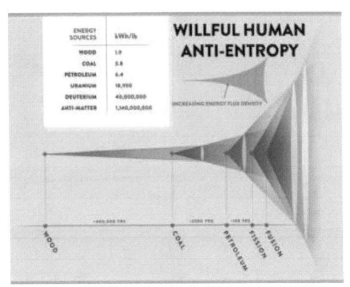

If you're not progressing you're dying. The above illustration of the anti-entropic tendency of a healthy human economy must be informed by the fact of the interconnected relationship of the energy flux density of heat used to accomplish work to the power of society to sustain greater creative activity at ever higher rates of production. This is the only metric of determining value and the basis of the anti-monetarist American System.

The fact is that while the Atlantic economies have currently submitted to the City of London- Wall Street and Troika demands for policies of depopulation, austerity through bail-outs and now bail-ins, Russia and China are committed to true development. Both countries are intent on creating a unified block of win-win cooperation based upon the Shanghai Cooperation Organization (SCO), Eurasian Economic Union and BRICS and that intention is based on anti-Malthusian scientific and technological progress. The Belt and Road Initiative which now involves over 66 countries exemplifies this spirit.

The financial system of the trans-Atlantic is collapsing and Putin knows it. Other Eurasian leaders know this. These leaders know that this is why a military bombardment of Syria had to be stopped and this is why Putin risked so much to expose the fraudulent claims that Syria had used chemical weapons and, along with China, vetoed the war hawks in the U.N. Security Council.

The current Eurasian economic block led by Russia and China expresses a unique commitment to scientific and technological progress, and if western societies should wish to have any claim to being morally fit to survive, then this is an optimistic power that we must re-awaken in ourselves fast. For it is only by acting on principles of scientific discovery and progress that a proper perspective can be discovered to overcome the current obstacles to our survival. That is, the discovery of what the future can and must become IF a creative change is introduced into the system.

The only pathway to avoiding the collapse of the financial system and a thermonuclear war with Russia and China is to be found in imposing Natural Law vigorously upon the claimed "debts" which Wall Street, and the City of London wishes to have bailed out. The expression of this Natural Law takes the form of the restoration of Glass-Steagall laws across the trans-Atlantic economies, eliminating the $700 trillion debt bomb before it explodes and returning to the principles of national banking for all countries. Under such a reform and by joining in common interest with other nations in the Eurasian zone, a commitment to progress and security can be realized, and such poisonous cocktails as the TPP, CETA and NAFTA can be dumped forever.

Escaping the British two-sided trap of monetarism and ecologism means increasing the energy-flux density of society by going to fusion energy, space exploration, and mining the moon for Helium-3 as China is already preparing to do. The applications of a forward-looking space age society using fusion power, involves not only rendering imperial wars for oil and water obsolete (as energy and water will be made both incommensurably cheap and abundant relative to the fossil fuel based system now defining society's limits), but gives mankind the tools to green deserts, build great projects, create a system of Asteroid Defense and construct the long-overdue Bering Strait Tunnel, a key link in the

World Land Bridge. These are the sorts of long term projects which not only remind us of our common self interests, but as JFK described the space program in 1962, create goals which "will serve to organize and measure the best of our energies and skills".

This is the future that we can still unleash at this most opportune time of world crisis.

Notes

[1] The UN Security Council was still based upon principles of national sovereignty as the basis for international law, and featured both America, Britain and Russia as VETO-wielding members.

[2] Bloomfield's Montreal-based Permindex operations were discovered by former D.A. of New Orleans Jim Garrison to be at the center of the assassination of John F. Kennedy. The full story is told here.

FROM THE ARCHIVES:

CHINA PUTS SURVIVAL OF CANADA-SINO "SPECIAL RELATIONSHIP" (DEC. 2017)

Ever since Canadian Prime Minister Justin Trudeau landed in Beijing for the inaugural Dialogue of World Parties Conference on December 3, mainstream press from all sides of the aisle have been echoing shock over the failure of the highly publicized trip which was heralded as being the long-awaited finalization of China's participation in the "Canada-China Free Trade Deal". This "deal" was not only designed to remove tariffs between countries in order to establish a Canada-China "special relationship", but also slip in "gender, climate change, good governance and labor" protocols which were strategically designed to bring China back onto the leash of Anglo-American liberal controlling influence.

While it appeared for some time that China was moving dangerously close to accepting this Free Trade deal which was crafted in an obsolete age of Obama-era geopolitics, the unceremonious treatment which Trudeau received upon arrival in China- which included a cancellation of a scheduled press conference, outright rejection of all of Canada's liberal demands by Premier Li Keqiang, and China's backing out of its promised partnership in the Canada-UK-China "Anti-Coal Alliance" indicates that China will no longer tolerate the British Empire's geopolitical games in any form.

The Canadian establishment voice of the National Post aptly observed in complete frustration:

It was always hard to see how Xi's vision which is illiberal to the extreme, squared with Trudeau's Ultra-liberal agenda. That they were irreconcilable should have been apparent before Monday."

But... the Trans Pacific Partnership was never meant to Die!

At this juncture, it must be noted that Canada's role as a "Middle Power" chess piece established with the first Prime Minister Trudeau's "counter-weight strategy" has become increasingly exposed for all to see. That is all, except those Anglo-American authors of this obsolete geopolitical trade deal. Those authors designed this trap specifically for a world in which the China-isolating Trans Pacific Partnership (TPP) was never killed by a Trump administration which itself was never meant to happen (1). It was designed for a fantasy world in which Syria was annihilated, Russia subdued, and isolated China brought to its knees, so desperate for resources that it would gladly adopt a Canada honey pot of cheap oil and resources... for a price. That price? That China remain under the grips of an Anglo American Unilateral governance structure subject to the whims of an elite that never learnt the lessons of Rome's downfall.

In former Cold War Days, when the world was broken more evenly into two opposing centers of gravity, such an Anglo-Canadian policy of shifting alliances between capitalist and communist powers at the expediency of the London-based players of the "Great Game", served a use for the Empire. Befriending Cuba, or China one day and the USA the next was the special role assigned to bi-polar British Canada. Today, with Trump's strategic alliance maturing between the USA and China and the fully matured Russo-Sino special relationship we are now at the cornerstone of new global paradigm, rendering this old formula obsolete, although the game masters of the old paradigm will not admit it.

A New Era of Win-Win Cooperation

While the current policy outlook of the Canadian political establishment is unfortunately committed to advancing the "old paradigm" agenda of zero-growth post-industrialism, manifested in these desperate attempts to induce China to return into the cage of the British Great Game- there is another Canada which China would love to work with as a partner and friend. This is the Canada that acts not in the interest of a sociopathic elite, but in the interest of the wellbeing of its citizens and humanity more generally. This is a Canada which seeks to join the Belt and Road Initiative now sweeping the globe and lifting billions out of poverty along the way. This would mean a revolutionary sweeping away of geopolitical thinking dominant since the Diefenbaker/JFK era ended. It would mean a revival of agro-industrial growth, centered around high speed rail, water, energy and space development, not to mention the long awaited opening up of the arctic in alignment with the decades old grand vision of Lyndon and Helga LaRouche.

As the Chinese Ambassador to Canada Lu Shaye stated in the wake of the historic May 2017 Belt and Road Conference in Beijing;

Canada could absolutely be an important participant, contributor, and beneficiary of the Belt and Road construction. Canada has joined the AIIB, which makes for good conditions for Canada to participate in the Belt and Road infrastructure construction. It is hoped that Canada could enhance policy coordination with Belt and Road countries, and seek specific areas and projects that it can take part in as soon as possible so as to gain early achievements through early participation.

The government of British Columbia signed the Belt and Road cooperation documents with China's Guangdong provincial government last year. We hope that the two local governments will take quick actions and actively participate in the construction.

China is also willing to cooperate with Canada to jointly explore the third-party markets under the Belt and Road initiative. The initiative responds to the trend of the times, conforms to the law of development, and meets the people's interests. It surely has broad prospects. I hope Canada will not miss any important opportunities for cooperation."

So with such a bright future clearly in view and with such great nations as Russia, China, India, Pakistan, and now even the United States getting on board, what are we waiting for exactly?

Notes

(1) The Trans-Pacific Partnership was designed as a "NAFTA of the Pacific" which served the two-fold purpose of 1) creating a legal basis for corporate dominance of sovereign nations caught in its web while keeping the USA in a dominant geopolitical position over Asia, and 2) isolating China from 12 key neighboring Pacific nations. This agenda was advanced as a parallel measure to Obama's 2011 "Pivot to Asia" military containment strategy of China also known by thinking analysts as the "Thucydides Trap"

THE ORIGINS OF THE DEEP STATE IN NORTH AMERICA PART II

Milner's Perversion Takes over Canada

"As between the three possibilities of the future: 1. Closer Imperial Union, 2. Union with the U.S. and 3. Independence, I believe definitely that No. 2 is the real danger. I do not think the Canadians themselves are aware of it... they are wonderfully immature in political reflection on the big issues, and hardly realize how powerful the influences are... On the other hand, I see little danger to ultimate imperial unity in Canadian 'nationalism'. On the contrary I think the very same sentiment makes a great many especially of the younger Canadians vigorously, and even bumptuously , assertive of their independence, proud and boastful of the greatness and future of their country, and so forth, would lend themselves, tactfully handled, to an enthusiastic acceptance of Imperial unity on the basis of 'partner-states'. This tendency is, therefore, in my opinion rather to be encouraged, not only as safeguard against 'Americanization', but as actually making, in the long run, for a Union of 'all the Britains'." [1]

-Lord Alfred Milner, 1909

Prologue

Canada's history has remained clouded in misinformation and outright lies for over 200 years, while basic truths which were once well understood by leading statesmen in Canada a century past are now treated as little more than myth or "conspiracy theory". Yet as the above quote written by the pen of Lord Alfred Milner indicates, the crafting of the Canadian identity has been bought for the price of a national soul. The greatest obstacle to Canadian sovereignty today is found in the fact that Canada's synthetic identity has been constructed over the past decades with the intention of obstructing the establishment upon this earth of a world of sovereign republics, which was and still is the outgrowth of the success of the American Revolution. To do so, we must investigate how the Anglo Dutch oligarchy has played through such institutions as the Rhodes Trust, Fabian Society, and Round Table Movement. These structures have played a key role in mis-shaping every key standard of economic, political, cultural and scientific behaviour which defines the Canadian System and associated identity to this day.

Part one of our story focused upon the creation of these institutions, and their methods of penetrating their networks throughout influential institutions of Canada from 1865 to 1943, and the evolution of the Round Table into the Royal Institute for International Affairs (RIIA) in 1919. American branches were created in 1920 with the Council on Foreign Relations and Institute of Pacific Relations, while a Canadian branch was established in 1928 with the Canadian Institute for International Affairs (CIIA). Key Canadian patriots resistant to the RIIA's plans were also introduced in the form of "Laurier Liberals" O.D. Skelton and Ernest Lapointe, both of whom aided in influencing the highly malleable Prime Minister William Mackenzie King towards the Canadian nationalist cause, greater cooperation with American Patriots such as Franklin Roosevelt and away from the RIIA's plans for world government under the League of Nations. With the mysterious deaths of Skelton and Lapointe in 1941, all such resistance melted away and Canadian foreign policy become fully infected by Rhodes Trust/ Fabian agents of the CIIA.

This second segment will address the important 1943-1972 destruction of humanist potential leading up to the reforms implemented by CIIA-assets Lester B. Pearson and Pierre Elliot Trudeau in their role in advancing Milner's program for a new synthetic nationalism.

The Attack on Post-War Potential Begins 1945-1951

By the end of the war, Canada's productive capacity had risen to unimaginable heights and the vision of unbounded progress free of imperial monetarism was not far off from realization. The relationship between Canada and the United States was at an all-time high, with exploding trade, and purchasing power that had multiplied threefold from 1939 to 1956. The authority and power won by C.D. Howe was continued into the following 12 years of Canadian progress first, as Minister of Reconstruction (1944-1948) then as Minister of Trade and Commerce (1948-1957). When Howe realized that his resistance to Canada's participation in the unjust Korean war of 1950 would not work, he changed gears, and took advantage of the situation by renewing his broad war powers, once again allowing himself to lead Canada's economy top down, resulting in the great projects with America such as the St Lawrence Seaway, the Avro Arrow CF-105 supersonic interceptor, the TransCanada-U.S. natural gas pipeline and especially the civilian use of nuclear power shaped by Canada's unique CANDU technology. [2]

The amazing rise in Canada's productive powers of labour by the end of WWII were largely due to the scientific leadership of the founders and managers of the NRC and AECL such as E.W.R Steacy [left], C.D. Howe [middle] and C.J. Mackenzie [right]

The secret to Canada's progress during and after the war continued to be the National Research Council (NRC), re-organized and rehabilitated after years of incompetence under its former President General Andrew McNaughton. The NRC was a flexible top down organization run by one of Howe's brightest engineering students C.J. Mackenzie who went on to become the first President of Atomic Energy Canada Ltd (AECL).

With similar mission-oriented organizational structures having organically formed in the USA during war, the NRC was celebrated and studied as a model for countries the world over. The leaders of this institution fought not only to advance nuclear power in Canada in order to escape the limits of fossil fuels and accelerate the next breakthrough to thermonuclear fusion, but also led the fight to provide their technology to underdeveloped countries such as India and Pakistan which were yearning to break free of their British colonial masters [3]. The NRC also successfully led breakthroughs in radio astronomy, oceanography and industry. Its basic objective can be summarized in the following model:

(1) Maximize the density of discoveries within a cross country system of self-financed and self-organized intramural NRC laboratories.

(2) Translate those discoveries into new technological applications and machine tools.

(3) Apply these technologies as efficiently as possible into the industrial productive system to increase the productive powers of labour.

(4) Force university curricula and behaviour to adapt by such creative upshifts as quickly as possible ensuring that no fixed/formulaic patterns of thought could encrust themselves upon the minds of students or professors.

Dexter White and Wallace

The Cultural/Economic/Scientific factors of Canada's post-war dynamic were on a new trajectory of true independence, founded on a commitment to progress which the British Empire now mobilized all of its energy to destroy. The great fear of Lord Milner laid out in 1909 of "union with the United States" guided by unbounded scientific and technological progress was now underway, peaking with a 1948 call for a North American customs union

Harry Dexter White [left] and Henry Wallace [right] were among the targets of McCarthy's "socialist" witch hunt during the Cold War.

advocated by Howe and leading FDR statesmen in the United States that had not yet been purged by the Cold War witch hunt led by Senator McCarthy. Sadly, now under the vast influence of the British Empire's mind control, one of Mackenzie King's last acts in office was the destruction of this proposition. After King's 1950 death, C.D. Howe continued on as Minister of Trade and Commerce under King's successor Louis St. Laurent (1948-1957) [4].

Having ensured that FDR's postwar vision for a world of sovereign nation states would not come to fruition after his untimely death in April 1945, the first of a series of ideological barrages was hammered into Canadian and U.S. policy beginning with the installation of Wall Street tool Harry Truman as President, and with him the advent of the "Truman Doctrine" centering on the Rhodes-Milner agenda of Anglo-American Empire guided by Churchill's design of "British brains and American brawn". While FDR was still alive, his allies led by Harry Dexter White and Henry Wallace were capable of fending off John Maynard Keynes' attempts to structure the Bretton Woods

Here Anglophile President Harry S Truman walks in gleeful bliss with his handler Sir Winston Churchill

agreements according to his own twisted logic of a one world currency steered by the Nazi affiliated Bank for International Settlements and Bank of England (of which Keynes was a Director). However, after FDR's death, the last major beachhead of resistance to British recolonization melted.

The Anglo-American "special relationship" was quickly established by Truman bringing American foreign policy quickly under the control of the RIIA networks beginning with Truman's unnecessary utilization of two of America's only three nuclear bombs on the already defeated Japan which set the foundations for the Korean War [5]. This policy was ushered in by Sir Winston Churchill's 1946 "Iron Curtain" speech in Fulton, Missouri which officially opened the age of the Cold War, setting a fear based dynamic of tension that resulted in a purging of FDR allies from positions of influence, and an influx of British operatives into high prominence the world over.

The Chicago Tribune's Cassandra Sounds the Alarm

In 1951, the enormously influential Massey-Lévesque Royal Commission attempted to first launch an attack upon the "American invasion" of media (print, radio, television and cinema) which was taking over the Canadian psyche. One of the primary demands of the 1951 report called for an emergency ban on U.S. media to keep "dangerous" American cultural influences from contaminating Canada's British traditions with the following words:

"Few Canadians realize the extent of this dependence... our lazy, even abject imitation of them [American institutions] has caused an uncritical acceptance of ideas and assumptions which are alien to our tradition". [6]

What were these types of alien ideas which concerned the British Empire so much at this important period of historical change? To get a sense of the fear which Massey and his British masters felt regarding the "low brow" American journalism being read by Canadians, it is useful to take a sample of a 1951 article written by journalist Eugene Griffin "Canada Offers Fine Field to Rhodes' Wards" published as one of a series of 16 explosive articles between July 15-31 in the Chicago Tribune:

"Scholars and other British educated Canadians are in a unique position to serve Britain through Canada's influence on Washington as a next door neighbour of the United States. Canada acts as a connecting link between England and the United States, helping to hold the neighbouring republic in line with the dominion's mother country... When Gen. MacArthur displeased Britain and Canada by his efforts to win the Korean war, Canada's Oxford educated minister for external affairs, Lester B. Pearson, complained that American-Canadian relations had become "difficult and delicate". MacArthur was fired the next day... Pearson's foreign office staff is packed with Rhodes scholars. There are 23 among 183 staff officers, or one out of every eight, who were educated at Oxford university, England, on the scholarships created by Cecil Rhodes, empire builder and diamond mogul who wanted the United States taken back into Britain's fold [see Box]... Other Canadian foreign office members also were educated in England, although not as Rhodes scholars. Pearson went to Oxford (St. John's, 1922) on a Massey scholarship, endowed by a Canadian millionaire... Norman A. Robertson, a Rhodes Scholar (Balliol, 1923) sometimes called the most brilliant member of the British trained inner circle in the government's East Block, headquarters of the prime minister and the foreign office, is another important figure in Canada's relations with Britain and the United States. He is clerk of the Privy Council and Secretary to the cabinet, and has been undersecretary of state and High Commissioner to Britain."

Little could the writers of the Chicago Tribune then know that during the very summer of their writing, a young Fabian, having just returned home from his conditioning under Harold Laski's mentorship at the London School of

Rhodes Scholars Penetrate Canada

Vincent Massey   Norman Robertson   Jack Pickersgil   Arnold Heeney

Cecil Rhodes   Lester B. Pearson   Escott Reid   F.R. Scott   Hume Wrong

By 1951, large and influential nests of Oxford-trained Rhodes scholars had infested vast branches of government and academia through efforts led by Lord Alfred Milner protégé Vincent Massey and his pet, Lester B. Pearson. Pictured above is a small coterie of the most insidious Rhodes scholars referred to in the 1951 Chicago Tribune article, with Cecil Rhodes seated at left.

Such operatives as Pierre Trudeau [left], Marc Lalonde [middle] and Gerard Pelletier [right] all got their start simultaneously as recruits in Ottawa's Privy Council Office under the watch of Rhodes Scholar Norman Robertson

Economics was working at his first job in the Privy Council Office (PCO) under the watch of Rhodes Scholar and Privy Council Clerk Norman Robertson. That young Fabian went by the name Pierre Elliot Trudeau [7]. Working alongside Trudeau at the time in the PCO included his supervisor Gordon Robertson, a young Oxford man named Marc Lalonde and his friend Gerard Pelletier, all three of whom went on to play prominent roles in Trudeau's powerful inner cabal 20 years later.

Upon returning to Montreal in 1951, Trudeau came under the control of F.R. Scott, Rhodes Scholar and co-founder of the League of Social Reconstruction (LSR) 20 years earlier. Trudeau's celebrity as an enemy of Quebec Premier Maurice Duplessis was cultivated by these Rhodes networks through his publication Cité Libre which served to 1) brainwash young intellectuals according to the journal's existential Catholic "personalist" philosophy of French philosophers Jacques Maritain and Emmanuel Mounier on the one side and 2) rally a populist attack on the Vatican-influenced Union Nationale (UN) government of Duplessis, Daniel Johnson Sr. and Paul Sauvé on the other [8]. This provincial government had made its renown not only for resisting British control over its destiny, but had also been a beachhead of resistance against eugenics laws then being implemented across the continent [9]. Trudeau worked in tandem with the creepy network of social engineers run from Laval University by Father George Henri Lévesque (co-chair of the Massey Commission), which exploded onto the scene in 1960 as the "Quiet Revolution" overthrow of the Union

Nationale after two untimely heart attacks of UN leaders beginning with Duplessis in 1959, then followed by Paul Sauvé a mere nine months later.

Another personality whose celebrity was being created in tandem with Trudeau's during the 1950s included Trudeau`s schoolboy chum, and British Intelligence asset René Lévesque, whose popular CBC radio show Point de Mire served to rally public opinion against the Duplessis regime and prepare the culture for the radically liberalizing reforms of the Quiet Revolution [10].

Huxley's UNESCO Doctrine and Eugenics

The guidelines for the post-1945 path to a New World Order were laid out clearly by Sir Julian Huxley in his 1946 **UNESCO: Its Purpose and Its Philosophy:**

Sir Julian Huxley founded UNESCO in order to make the science of eugenics become a standard of social control under a new name.

"The moral for UNESCO [United Nations Education, Science and Cultural Organization] is clear. The task laid upon it of promoting peace and security can never be wholly realised through the means assigned to it- education, science and culture. It must envisage some form of world political unity, whether through a single world government or otherwise, as the only certain means of avoiding war... in its educational programme it can stress the ultimate need for a world political unity and familiarize all peoples with the implications of the transfer of full sovereignty from separate nations to a world organization." [11]

To what end would this "world political unity" be aimed? Several pages later, Huxley's vision is laid out in all of its twisted detail:

"At the moment, it is probable that the indirect effect of civilization is dysgenic instead of eugenic, and in any case it seems likely that the dead weight of genetic stupidity, physical weakness, mental instability and disease proneness, which already exist in the human species will prove too great a burden for real progress to be achieved. Thus even though it is quite true that any radical eugenic policy will be for many years politically and psychologically impossible, it will be important for UNESCO to see that the eugenic problem is examined with the greatest care and that the public mind is informed of the issues at stake so that much that is now unthinkable may at least become thinkable." [12]

How could "the unthinkable" application of a practice which Hitler had made repulsive to humanity, become adopted by a society which had a faith in progress and unbounded creativity so incompatible with social Darwinism? Huxley's own life's decision to become a founding member of the World Wildlife Fund (WWF) in 1961 alongside Bilderberg Group founder Prince Bernhard and Prince Philip provides us a clue. It is no coincidence that Huxley's role as President of the British Eugenics Society (1959-1962) also overlapped his co-creation of the World Wildlife Fund (WWF).

Club of Rome founders Alexander King [left] and Aurelio Peccei [right] were both unapolo-getic Malthusians who sought to establish the language of 'systems analysis' to prove that man-kind was condemned to destruction unless world government and population reduction were not made global policy

The only way such a genocidal policy as eugenics, masquerading as "objective" science, could be readopted by humanity was through the dissociation of mind from matter, via the breaking of "subjective values" from "objective facts". The method chosen was a worshipping of the ugly and irrational in the aesthetics such that judgement could no longer be governed by a sense of truth and beauty, while the "cold and logical" was separated from the artistic and kept in its own cold dark mechanical universe accessible only through statistical methods of thought. This is how the modern school system has been divided into two different synthetic worlds of Arts and Sciences. The operatives chosen to carry out this policy were Massey's ally Sir Kenneth Clark and Sir John Maynard Keynes who led the scientific management of culture in Britain [13]. The mental cage chosen to schism "values" from "facts" in managing human affairs was named "systems analysis".

A major goal of the Massey Commission and its UNESCO design, was to create structures that would elevate the Humanities and Social Sciences to the highest pedestal of knowledge (and financing), paving the road for the later acceptance of systems 8-a-Club of Rome King Peccei analysis to be used in the management of society. The person assigned to impose "systems" planning into political practice was the Lord President of the British Empire's Scientific Secretariat Alexander King working through the Organization for European Economic Cooperation (OEEC), (later to become the Organization of Economic Cooperation and Development (OECD) in 1961). Under the OECD, King became Director General of Scientific Affairs and went on to co-found the Malthusian Club of Rome alongside Italian industrialist Aurelio Peccei in 1968 [14].

The CIIA's Royal Commissions Deconstruct and

Reconstruct the Synthetic Soul of Canada

The RIIA directed its various branches, and Rhodes Trust networks around the world to implement the New Eugenics project outlined by Julian Huxley in 1946. In Canada, the implementation process occurred between an intervals of 24 years and took the form of four CIIA-directed operations whose immense influence cannot be overstated. They were:

1) The Royal Commission into the Arts and Letters (1949-1951),

2) The Royal Commission on Economic Prospects for Canada (1955-1957),

3) The Royal Commission on Government Organization (1960-1963), and

4) The Senate Committee on Science Policy (1968-1972).

Each commission was designed with the effect of establishing new structures of thought upon policy makers in the domain of culture, economic and science policy which induced the blind acceptance of satanic policies of Malthusian eugenics masquerading as "environmentalism", or the "science" of saving nature from civilization. A society imbued with a moral sense of Judeo-Christian ethic and love of progress, and strengthened by the Roosevelt-led fight against Hitler, would never accept Eugenics. A fact well known to the Anglo-Dutch oligarchy.

A Royal Commission, as the name implies is an invention of the British Empire which has been used for centuries in order to create the perception that top down structural changes in all aspects of government were "scientifically" and objectively achieved. The truth is that conclusions of such Commissions have always been pre-decided by the ruling oligarchy long before the Royal Commission's experts were even formed. Usually spanning 2-3 years of studies by a clique of pre-selected "experts" in a given field, Royal Commissions produce voluminous data sets, hundreds of thousands of pages of information, and then summarize their findings and prescriptions in the form of several summary reports consisting of a 1-2 thousand pages. The sheer quantity of data associated with such reports is supposed to dissuade anyone from giving any respect to other countervailing opinion which challenge the Commission's findings, with the assumption that unless everyone commits two years of their lives to a specialized study funded by millions of dollars and thousands of man hours, then their opinion could not be worth anything.

The Massey-Lévesque Commission: The First Wave of Attack 1949-1951

In Canada, Milner-protégé Vincent Massey was assigned the unique responsibility of leading the implementation of this multifaceted program which struck in a series of Royal Commissions organized entirely by agents of the CIIA. Massey's role was carried out as the chairman of the already mentioned Royal Commission on National Development in the Arts, Letters and Sciences (1949-1951) alongside his co-chairman Father George Henri Lévesque, a social scientist and Dominican priest who is rightly credited as the intellectual godfather of the 1960-1966 "Quiet Revolution" which secularized the province of Quebec and brought in OECD educational reforms. All proposals sought by the end of this two year study were directed by the UNESCO agenda which Sir Julian Huxley laid out publicly in 1946 [15].

As Massey's former assistant Karen Finlay wrote in The Force of Culture: Vincent Massey and Canadian Sovereignty, Massey's lifelong governing principle was ***"principle of disinterest"*** whereby Massey argued that it is "intellectual detachment" which empowers someone to truly judge the aesthetic value of art [16]. Under the logic of UNESCO and Massey's satanic formula, it is assumed that since personal "subjective" values pollute one's judgements on "the beautiful and good', it is only by disassociating oneself from pre-existing values, that we gain the ability to judge "good" and "bad" art in an "objective" and thus "true" fashion.

The severing of the subjective from the objective thusly also forces the denial of any pre-existing standards by which anything could be judged as intrinsically good or bad, and thus a ripe field of moral relativism can be harvested. Evil may then run wild without any fear of being challenged. In other words, this is a complete denial of the existence of universal physical principles

The structures against universal physical principles which were proscribed in the Massey-Lévesque Commission involved the creation of a more powerful Canadian Broadcasting Corporation, a National Film Board, a National Library, a National Art Gallery, a National Art Bank, a Social Sciences and Humanities Research Council, Federal financing of the education system in the humanities and social sciences, and Canada Council for the Arts modelled on Keynes' semi-autonomous, government financed British template [17].

The Federal financing of the education system was vital for the Commission since it was the only way which OECD and UNESCO reforms could be ushered in without provincial resistance. Pre-existing teaching practices emphasizing the Greek Classics, which treated students as if they had a soul, could only be dismantled efficiently under this top down restructuring, applied during the 1960s in which moral relativism, Darwinism, and "new math" increasingly replaced anything of substance. The horrendous explosion of modernist, abstract and banal art generously sponsored under the structures of Massey's Canada Council (f.1957) gives one a sick sense of the spiritual disease with which the imperialists (and sadly their victims) are infected. Both federal control of education and the arts were necessary to pervert the principles guiding both, and establish the mental/spiritual infrastructure supportive of satanic programs of Malthusian population reduction as the new environmentalist eugenics was designed to be.

To amplify this spiritual disease, the Massey-Levesque Commission even proscribed the creation of a Canadian honours system such that oligarchical habits could more easily be cultivated in Canada [18]. The creation of the

Canada Council took much longer than Massey would have liked, and its postponement was due largely to the resistance of the l'Union Nationale government of Quebec and its Vatican-steered Catholic Church. The powerful elements within the Quebec Catholic Church were among the only organized forces on the continent that had competently identified the satanic intentions underlying the OECD-UNESCO reforms being infiltrated into global educational and political systems.

It were for such reasons that Father Lévesque and his ideological offspring of social engineers and technocrats at the University Laval had become the bitter enemies of the Union Nationale government. The implementation of OECD educational reforms as prescribed by the Massey-Lévesque Commission were a primary focus of the Quiet Revolution. The task of applying the reforms was given in large part to two Rhodes Scholars: Jean Beetz and the creator of the Quebec Ministry of Education, Paul Gérin-Lajoie. Soon-to-become Prime Minister Pierre Elliot Trudeau played a key institutional role in this process as well in the Law Faculty at University Laval alongside Lalonde and Beetz.

With the creation of the Canada Council, the "scientific management" of culture, so necessary to elevate the ugly and banal into a position of respectable authority was ensured and the ground was thus laid for the next steps of the fascist takeover of Canada.

The Gordon Commission: The Second Wave of Attack 1955-1957

"Many Canadians are worried about such a large degree of economic decision-making being in the hands of non-residents [because it] might lead to economic domination by the United States and eventually to the loss of our political independence."

-1957 Gordon Commission Report [19]

The Massey-Lévesque Commission was followed systematically, by the Royal Commission on the Economic Prospects of Canada (1955-1957) chaired by Walter Lockhart Gordon, chairman of the National Executive Committee of the CIIA and head of the largest accounting firm in Canada Clarkson-Gordon Management. The Commission claimed that Canada's sovereignty was threatened by American ownership of Canadian enterprise, and that drastic action to cut America off from the Canadian economy were absolutely necessary.

As historian Stephen Azzi demonstrated in his 2007 study Foreign Investment and the Paradox of Economic Nationalism [20], the claims made by the report were entirely fraudulent. The massive upshift in quality of life, electricity and social services due to American capital in Canada was not even addressed in the voluminous Gordon

Commission reports. Thus the only relevant purpose of the report was to cultivate a culture of anti-Americanism, and establish political structures limiting foreign ownership of Canadian markets, and lower the potential living conditions of Canadians [21]. The biggest farce embedded in the Gordon Commission quote above, of course, which Azzi misses, is that there never was any political independence for Canada to lose to Americans in the first place, since it had never freed itself from the political and economic clutches of its British Mother.

Gordon went onto implement his own proposals after leading the cleansing of the Liberal Party of all C.D. Howe Liberals between 1957-1963 [22], becoming Finance Minister (1963-65) under his long-time puppet-on-loan from Vincent Massey, Lester Pearson, whom he himself selected as early as 1955 to run for leadership of the Liberal Party [23]. After his policies as Finance Minister failed, Gordon took over the post of President of the powerful Privy Council Office (1966-68) from his predecessor Maurice Lamontagne.

These two commissions were designed to "sound the alarm bells" against Canadian vulnerability to an imminent American imperial takeover of Canada's culture and economic resources. Although no evidence was ever presented that American imperialism had any intention to take over Canada, the prescriptions to save Canada from economic and cultural Americanization involved both a negative and positive component: Negatively, each proposed the rapid implementation of quota systems/ tariff systems to limit foreign input of capital and media, while positively, proposing centralized structures to coordinate culture and economic management by a vast London-steered bureaucracy. The already long controlled mass media outlets of Canada glamorized their findings and created a mass fear in the popular culture.

The effect of these two reports also amplified anti-Americanism to such a feverish pitch that a Canadian identity could be established on a fear-based negation, whereby Massey, Lévesque and Gordon following the prescription laid out by Lord Milner in 1909 crafted a blueprint for a "New Nationalism". This counterfeit nationalism was wrapped up with a brand new national anthem and Canadian flag upon Lester B. Pearson's Liberals becoming the government in 1963.

The Delphic perception of Canada's sovereign status outside of the actual control of the British Empire had to be established for the next wave of Canada's post-1963 role in trapping nations into the imperial spider's web of International Monetary Fund conditionalities.

Unlike the flags of most countries, the noble Maple Leaf, as many Canadians have still yet to realize, has neither now nor ever signified anything whatsoever.

The Glassco Commission: The Third Wave of Attack
1960-1963

Once the Canadian cultural inferiority complex was amplified sufficiently by fear of American imperialism, the collective neurotic mindset was now ready for the next wave of the CIIA's onslaught unleashed with the Royal Commission on Government Organization (1960-1963) chaired by Walter Gordon's partner at Clarkson-Gordon, John Grant Glassco. Glassco was the son of William Grant, and nephew of Vincent Massey. This commission brought in a monetarist/accounting framework for managing a bureaucratic structure under the logic of *"letting managers manage"*. As its mission statement laid out: *"This report examines the adequacy of existing arrangements for making economic and statistical services available for the formulation of policy, for administrative decisions, and for the service and enlightenment of the public."* [24]

A little later, the report laid out the belief that all problems with inefficiency in achieving policy objectives was due to the fact that there are too few economists and social scientists in controlling administrative positions of government: *"..Very little can be done, or ought to be done, to discourage the movement of economists into higher administrative posts. Talented administrators are just as scarce as economists, and it would be a mistake for the public service to deny itself any fruitful source of good administrators."* [25]

In preparation for Finance Minister Walter Gordon's 1963-65 implementation of his 1957 Royal Commission financial proposals, Glassco laid out the new necessary controlling structures to allow Gordon to cut off Canada from American investments, and choke off as much of America from Canada as possible when he wrote: *"The immediate concern is the development of a competent central economic staff within the Department of Finance, not to take over work done elsewhere but rather, under the direction of the Minister of Finance, to attend to the development of general economic policy for the government as a whole ."* [26]

Finally, Glassco pushed for the UNESCO policy of amplifying the social sciences while attacking the "hard" sciences like physics and biology with the following: "The relatively slow development of economic research in Canadian universities, due to shortage of funds, bears on both the quantity and quality of the future supply of trained economists. While the government is spending scores of millions annually to support research in physics and biology, little financial assistance is given to research in the social sciences" [27]

The edict of "letting managers manage" was necessary if the appearance of democracy were to be maintained while the absolute control of society by an accounting priesthood was to be preserved. The commission's reports called for the adoption of "horizontal" (aka: bottom up) planning which was to replace the archaic belief in "vertical" (aka: top down) intentions from elected officials to the process they were elected to preside over, as was the common practice of the NRC and its administrators.

Ironically, while bottom up planning according to accounting standards was pushed, central control through the Treasury Board was also promoted by Glassco. This prescription would ensure that only a small coterie would ever fully have their minds on the whole, while every other department were too busy focusing on hyper-specialized compartmentalized parts to think about the whole.

While the NRC and its leadership such as C.J. Mackenzie, the student of the late C.D. Howe and the late Dr. E.W.R. Steacy were vigorously attacked by the Glassco Commission, the overhaul which Glassco prescribed involved the centralized planning of science policy according to budgetary constraints under the Treasury and a Science Secretariat. These positions were to become completely subservient to the control of bureaucrats specialized in accounting and monetary economics degrees advanced through the "social sciences and humanities" programs outlined by UNESCO. With this new system of management and its anal adherence to Planning-Programming-Budgeting (PPB), the problems associated with the governments such as those of C.D. Howe and later John Diefenbaker (1957-1963) which intended to actually get something done for the improvement of the nation, could not occur [28]. This systemic reform was not an end in and of itself however, and was merely a necessary stepping stone towards actualizing a system of thinking which would accept the linear language of "Systems Analysis" as a guide for conceptualizing the management of humanity under laws of entropy, constrained by the limits of fixed resources.

The Glassco Report's prescriptions for policy overhaul were to be implemented fully by Trudeau several years later.

As a reward for a job well done, Glassco was promoted from Executive Vice-President of Brazilian Traction, Light and Power Co. to President in 1963.Under this position, the overthrow of the nationalist Brazilian President João Goulart was effected via a military coup d'état [29]. The free market pillaging of Brazil created a model applied even more aggressively a decade later with Henry Kissinger's orchestration of the Pinochet regime's coup in Chile.

The Lamontagne Commission's 1967-1973 Program for Genocide

The last wave of this CIIA-run Milner Project for a new nationalism (at least insofar as major structural reforms were concerned), took the form of the Senate Special Committee on Science Policy (1967-1972), more popularly known as the Lamontagne Commission after its chairman Senator Maurice Lamontagne [30]. This commission had the distinction of being the most transparent in its satanic intention to ban creativity and impose Malthusian constraints un-naturally upon the management of human affairs. The report is especially relevant as it begins with the acknowledgement of the American System of Political Economy, which it then attempts to destroy by lies and ridicule:

Two hundred years after Benjamin Franklin [left] and his young protégé Alexander Hamilton [right] established the American System of Political Economy in order to ensure the success of the young Republic, the British Empire was still yearning to tear its existence from the books of history in order to establish a new world order.

"During the early part of the 19th century, Great Britain and to a lesser extent France were fast developing industrial technology and finding ways of fruitfully exploiting science. Later on the United States moved from technical backwardness to such a level that it could begin exporting to the "advanced" European countries manufacturing techniques and machine tools so different that the whole approach became known as the "American System". An English productivity team that visited the United States in 1853 to study this 'system' concluded that "men served God in America, in all seriousness and sincerity, through striving for economic efficiency." [31]

By identifying the fact of creativity's relationship to technological advance, and technological advance's relationship to increased growth and productivity, embedded self-consciously in the American System founded by U.S. Treasury Secretary Alexander Hamilton and his mentor Benjamin Franklin, Lamontagne, a student of George Henri Lévesque and key member of the Gordon Commission twelve years earlier, established his commitment to defend the principle of empire. The most active defender of the American System during the 20th and 21st century, Lyndon LaRouche (1922-2019) has subsequently described contrast between the forces active today the following terms:

"The most readily accessed example of the contrast of good to evil in modern times, has been typified not only by the goodness of the anti-monetarist principle on which the original Constitution of the United States of America was premised; it was also the same principle which had been adopted earlier by the Massachusetts Bay Colony. That principle, which modern society should trace back to such Renaissance geniuses as Nicholas of Cusa, has been demonstrated through the crucial quality of a leading contributing role specific to the included role of U.S. Treasury Secretary Alexander Hamilton." [32]

Lamontagne's allegiance to the monetarist forces opposing the American System, can be clearly seen when Lamontagne let his true intention shine forth when he wrote in vol. 2 of his 3 volume report:

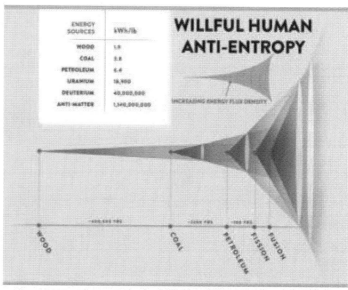

If you're not progressing you're dying. The above illustration of the anti-entropic tendency of a healthy human economy must be informed by the fact of the interconnected relationship of the energy flux density of heat used to accomplish work to the power of society to sustain greater creative activity at ever higher rates of production. This is the only metric of determining value and the basis of the anti-monetarist American System.

"It is becoming apparent, however, that nature is not as passive as we thought, that it has its own laws and can revenge itself, once its own equilibrium has been disrupted... Nature imposes definite constraints on technology itself and if man persists in ignoring them the net effect of his action in the long run can be to reduce rather than to increase nature' potential as a provider of resources and habitable space... But then, an obvious question arises: How can we stop man's creativeness?" [33]

Thus, Lamontagne has established that it is man's creativity itself that must be stopped if the supposed "fixed" equilibrium of nature will remain unchanged by technology! This is the root morality of the current global environmentalist religion which Lamontagne was at the forefront of unleashing. Since Lamontagne admits that his "ideal" solution of destroying man's creative impulse is itself an impossibility, like the Zeus of Aeschylus's Prometheus Bound, he never the less finds a resolution to this problem by introducing a perverse alternative when he wrote:

"How can we proclaim a moratorium on technology? It is impossible to destroy existing knowledge; impossible to paralyze man's inborn desire to learn, to invent and to innovate... In the final analysis we find that technology is merely a tool created by man in pursuit of his infinite aspirations and is not the significant element invading the natural environment. It is material growth itself that is the source of conflict between man and nature" [32]

Thus creativity and its fruits of technological progress are acceptable only IF they reduce the assumed conflict between man and nature posited by Lamontagne! "Bad" technology in Lamontagne's formulation, has the effect of increasing humanity's powers of productivity and thus increase the entropy in his fixed ecosystem-based economy. If, on the other hand, we promote technologies of a low energy flux density form, such as windmills, solar panels and biodiesel, which lead to the reduction of man's powers to exist, then technology can be defined as a "good" thing.

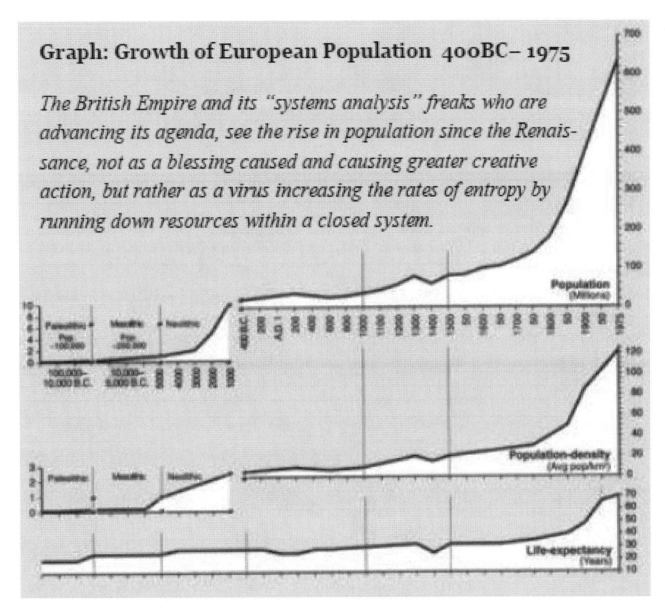

Graph: Growth of European Population 400BC–1975

The British Empire and its "systems analysis" freaks who are advancing its agenda, see the rise in population since the Renaissance, not as a blessing caused and causing greater creative action, but rather as a virus increasing the rates of entropy by running down resources within a closed system.

This is the genocidal intention of the British Empire expressed in all its nakedness, which has been the primary target of American statesman and founder of the science of Physical Economy, Lyndon LaRouche. By the time of the Lamontagne Commission, LaRouche had already risen to world prominence as the only effective challenger to the British monarchy's genocidal agenda of lowering the energy flux density underlying society's material and intellectual existence. LaRouche has subsequently fought for 50 years to defend the truth of mankind's scientifically verifiable relationship to the universe, as being governed by everything which Lamontagne and his Anglo-Dutch masters hate: mankind's necessity for unbounded scientific and technological progress expressed as the unending obligation to increase the productive powers of labour.

The concept which LaRouche has used to guide mankind's mandate for progress, is the increase of energy flux density of cycling of atoms through the biosphere and human economy, shaped by upgrades of new platforms of technologies. Compare LaRouche's view on energy-flux density with the cynical rubbish promoted expressed by Lamontagne above:

"The rates of increase of energy-flux density in the concentrations of increasing rates of intensity of power per capita, must be now be restarted, and also accelerated; otherwise, the death-rates throughout the world are now already accelerating at rates which must be identified as a global trend in planetary human genocide... The nominal trend in rising rates of genocide is not the only aspect of this threatening trend. The inability to maintain a correlated set of rates of increase of the energy-flux density of the human persons per capita, must be correlated with the falling rate of intellectual development of the typical U.S.A. or European citizen. The so-called "green doctrine" is a doctrine of practice which results in not only human genocide, but a decadence in the mental powers, and also the relative sanity, of the individual human being." [34]

What LaRouche is describing is the simple fact that without a constant increase of energy-flux density of the system and each individual within that system, then the domination by a green doctrine which sets "value" upon forms of energy and behaviour which reduce mankind's power to accomplish work is destined to exterminate the population trapped within that system. The effect of destroying the means to increase the energy flux density of the system (ie: Creativity) means that a policy of genocide is the only alternative for a ruling oligarchy!

How would such a logic of genocide be accepted by citizens and administrators who are animated by the inspired faith in scientific and technological progress as was still largely the case during the late 1960s? For this task, Lamontagne had already let the cat out of the bag when he wrote in vol. 1:

"If general science policy is to accomplish its crucial role effectively, it must also develop a system of control, to make sure that the strategy will be respected in the detailed decision-making process and review mechanisms... Perhaps more than any other sector of policy, science policy requires the careful application of systems analysis." [35]

With the linear language of systems analysis, the minds of those trying to manage any intrinsically non-linear process became sufficiently crippled with statistics and compartmentalization that their ability to see either 1) a whole top down process, or 2) the tragic consequences of their own foolish beliefs, was destroyed. Similar to the logic adopted ten years earlier with the state-run Canada Council which provided top down grants to "certain types" of art, music and social theories compatible to an oligarchy, though abhorrent to natural human sentiment, the Lamontagne Commission called passionately for a centralized financing and planning body in order to fund those "types" of applied technologies and pure research which were compatible with the genocidal aims of an oligarchy, but would never be accepted by a society imbued with even a little common sense and human compassion. In this spirit Lamontagne exclaimed that:

"The creation of a dynamic and balanced science organization is an urgent necessity. A main centre of coordination and financing of science policy is extremely desirable. The time has come to create a federal department of scientific affairs". [36]

Lamontagne is referring of course to the creation of the Canadian Ministry of State for Science and Technology (MOSST) which was modelled on the British system, and kept under the full control of the Treasury Board and its balanced accounting system. MOSST and the Treasury Board redirected Canadian science into the dark ages and its new emphasis on "ecosystems management" and "conservation" instead of nation building. The "new wisdom" advocated by Lamontagne demanded that science now be shackled to "market demand" instead of future orientation.

Enter Trudeau's Club of Rome

After the Rhodes Trust-directed ouster of the well intentioned, but incredibly naïve Conservative Prime Minister John Diefenbaker in 1963 [37], all of the measures proposed by these four Commissions were enforced vigorously by Lester B. Pearson and the Rhodes Trust/CIIA networks that had risen to prominence under him, and then fully by Pearson's replacement… the former Justice Minister Pierre Elliot Trudeau in 1968. Along with Trudeau came fellow CIIA-assets from the Privy Council Office Gerard Pelletier, and another disciple of Father Lévesque named Jean Marchand, both of whom were active with Trudeau's Cité Libre. The `new reformers` of Quebec became the `new reformers` of Canada.

Under Trudeau, the application of "systems analysis" as a cover for population reduction and fascism were fully carried into the top down management of government on all levels, and the Club of Rome of Alexander King, and his Canadian collaborators such as Maurice Strong, Maurice Lamontagne, Roland Mitchener (former Governor General) [38], Michael Pitfield (Personal Aid to Trudeau and head of Privy Council Office), Alastair Gillespie (Rhodes Scholar, and 1st MOSST), C.R. Nixon (Privy Council Office), Marc Lalonde (Rhodes Scholar, Trudeau advisor and head of Prime Ministers Office), Ronald Ritchie (National Advisor), Rennie Whitehead (Asst. Sec. to MOSST), and Ivan Head (head of Prime Minister`s Office) had set its putrid roots firmly into Canadian soil officially when the Canadian Branch was established informally in 1970 [39].

This nest was directly responsible for the creation of Environment Canada, which had applied systems analysis in order to transform what was once a policy of water and energy development, centred on a national mission, towards "ecosystems management". A strict dualism between civilized humanity characterized by change and the "unchanging pure equilibrium" of nature was assumed as law, and with this assumption, a new green religion arose masking its fascist intentions behind a "new Canadian nationalism" centred not around a love of freedom or development, but around a fear of both American and Russian aggressors and unfortunate admiration for Britain.

How the Present Comes from the Future: The Free Choice of the Will is a Matter of Mind

The lies of the past are looking pretty ugly. Shall we find the strength within ourselves as Canadians to look upon this disfigured ugliness which we are told is our heritage, in order to recapture the vision of Canada's sovereign potential as a great pioneering nation which held the imaginations of men such as Wilfrid Laurier, O.D. Skelton, C.D. Howe and John Diefenbaker? Shall we pick up upon the organic creative evolution that was so scarred and disfigured when Franklin Roosevelt died, and build such long overdue projects as the North American Water and Power Alliance, championed by the Kennedy brothers in the 1960s and Lyndon LaRouche today? Shall we rebuild our destroyed infrastructure along upgraded magnetic levitation train technology powered by advanced fourth generation nuclear thorium reactors and begin to taste the breakthrough of fusion? Shall we let go of the false genocidal notion of unchanging ecosystems and allow ourselves to see human beings as a species above and beyond everything else known in the biosphere, in that we are unique in our power to comprehend, and wilfully transform those processes of nature in a way that improves and speeds up their evolutionary progress towards ever higher states of energy-flux density?

That really depends on you.

Notes

(1) Milner to J.S. Sanders, 2 Jan. 1909 cited in "The Round Table Movement and Imperial Union" by John Kendle, University of Toronto Press, 1975, p.55

"(2) CANDU stands for CANadian Deuterium Uranium reactors which use heavy water (in which each atom of oxygen is combined with two atoms of the heavy isotope of hydrogen, deuterium) to slow the fast moving neutrons enough for appreciable absorption and splitting of the nuclei of unstable ("fissile") isotopes such as uranium-235, without the need to enrich the uranium-235 above its low natural abundance of 0.7 % relative to the non-fissile uranium-238. The absorption of neutrons by the nuclei of relatively stable "non-fissile" isotopes, such as the much more abundant isotopes uranium-238, or thorium-232, transmutes these heavy elements into the chemically distinct but fissile isotopes, plutonium-239 and uranium-233, which vastly expand the potential of nuclear power for mankind.

(3) Canadian scientists such as C.J. Mackenzie and E.W.R. Steacy were integral in shaping the Colombo Plan which served as a conduit in its early days for technology transfers to underdeveloped countries. After America, Canada was the 2nd country in the world to have civilian nuclear power in the form of its NRX research reactor. In the context of

President Dwight Eisenhower's 1953 "Atoms for Peace" program, Canada provided large scale transfers of its nuclear technology to developing countries., first to India, with a contract signed in April 1956 with the CIRUS research centre (constructed in 1960), and then soon after to Pakistan with the Karachi Nuclear Power Plant design supplied by G.E. Canada in 1966. Canada helped India construct two other reactors named RAPP-1 and RAPP-2, but contracts were soon ended for decades due to the creation of nuclear weapons by both countries as an effect of British-manipulated conflict. By the late 1960s, the emphasis on development was shifted from technology sharing and real nation building, towards external monetary aid, and "appropriate technologies" that wouldn't change the supposed "fixed cultural patterns" of indigenous peoples. In Canada this imperial re-orientation was overseen by Sir Maurice Strong who was assigned to create the Canadian International Development Agency (CIDA) in 1968 for this purpose.

(4) St. Laurent and Howe attempted to keep Canada's dynamic of growth and close relations with the United States as strong as possible throughout their time in office until they were overthrown in a CIIA-run coup of the Liberal Party. St. Laurent shared the Laurier Liberals' mistrust of the Rhodes Trust networks from an early point in his career, having been one of the first Québécois' to be offered the Rhodes scholarship in 1907, and rejected "the honour" favouring a Quebec-based education instead.

(5) L. Wolfe, The Beastmen Behind the Dropping of the Bomb, 21st Century Science and Technology, 2005

(6) Massey Report quote cited in Karen Finlay's "The Force of Culture: Vincent Massey and Canadian Sovereignty", University of Toronto Press, 2004, p. 218

(7) Trudeau had just returned to Canada from a 500 day long world tour instigated by Harold Laski, a recruiter of young talent and law professor at the London School of Economics who had mentored young Trudeau from 1947-49. Laski was also a leader of the Fabian Society at this time serving as the Head of the National Executive of the British Labour Party.

(8) Maritain and Mounier were part of the "Catholic" variety of the discrete collaborators with Vichy during WWII, after the integrist Pope, Pius XII, had signed a Concordat deal with Hitler. Maritain was an Ultramontane integrist type of fascist who revived Thomas Aquinas with the purpose of instituting a "New Middle Ages" with the collaboration of the Dominicans. Maritain and Mounier were the leaders of the very Catholic "Ordre Nouveau" under Vichy. (See Pierre Beaudry's Synarchy report on the DOMINICAN FASCIST YOUTH MOVEMENT in Book II: The Modern Synarchy Movement of Empire www.amatterofmind.org/Pierres_PDFs/SYNARCHY_I/BOOK_II/2._SYNARCHY_MOVEMENT_OF_EMPIRE_BOOK_II.pdf .) Maritain was the most important French philosopher of the war years in France and later in America. The entire Maritain, Mounier, and Reginald Garrigou-Lagrange salon at Meudon was anti- De Gaulle, during and after the war. They were "Catholic personalist communitarians" who oriented against individualism and materialism for the benefit of the Revolution Nationale of Petain.

(9) The March, 1946 issue of Eugenical News featured an article called "The Present Status of Sterilization Legislation in the United States" which demonstrates the eugenicists' anger with the Quebec Church: "The opposition of the Roman Catholic leaders constitutes the greatest obstacle that is encountered in applying, or in acquiring this therapeutic protection. From Maine come complaints that the Catholics of Quebec are moving southward and obstructing the proper use of their sterilization law. From Arizona we hear that no use has been made of their law 'because of religious objections.' Three States, Arizona, Arkansas, Nevada, have no institution for the feebleminded or epileptics, though some are cared for in the mental hospitals. Connecticut's population has a greater proportion of Catholics than any other State having a sterilization law. This accounts in part for the fact that only an occasional operation is being done there."

(10) Both Trudeau and Lévesque had prominent roles in the 1960-1966 operation with Trudeau working in the Institute for Research into Public Law under Rhodes Scholar Jean Beetz at Father Lévesque`s Université Laval and René Lévesque working as a Cabinet Minister of the Liberal government of Jean Lesage. For more on René Lévesque`s recruitment to British intelligence during WWII, see The Canadian Patriot #5, Feb. 2013.

(11) Julian Huxley: UNESCO Its Purpose and Its Philosophy, 1946, p.13

(12) Huxley, Ibid., p.21

(13) During the War, Britain had centralized its cultural control via the creation of the Council for the Encouragement of Music and Arts (CEMA) founded and led by the Director of Britain's National Art Gallery, Sir Kenneth Clark. Upon receiving his assignment after serving as fine arts curator at Oxford's satanic Ashmolean Museum, Clark was made Knight Commander of the Bath in 1938, one of the highest honours bestowed upon high ranking prostitutes of the oligarchy. After the war, CEMA became the Arts Council of Britain, chaired by John Maynard Keynes, a director of the British Eugenics Society until his death. Keynes is on record mere months before his death, exclaiming at a Galton Lecture in 1946 that eugenics is "the most important, significant and, I would add, genuine branch of sociology which exists" ["Opening remarks: The Galton Lecture". Eugenics Review vol 38 (1): 39–40.] These networks drove the counter-culture operation known as "The Congress for Cultural Freedom' (CCF)-sponsored by the Rockefeller Foundation, the CIA and directed by British Intelligence beginning in 1949. For more on the CCF, see The Congress for Cultural Freedom: Making the World Safe for Post-War Kulturkampf, by Jeff Steinberg and Steve Meyer, published in the June 24, 2004 issue of Executive Intelligence Review, downloadable on www.larouchepub.com

(14) In laying out the strategy for his life's work with the Club of Rome, King wrote in the forward to his 1991 book The First Global Revolution; "The common enemy of humanity is man. In searching for a new enemy to unite us, we came up with the idea that pollution, the threat of global warming, water shortages, famine and the like would fit the bill. All these dangers are caused by human intervention, and it is only through changed attitudes and behavior that they can be overcome. The real enemy then, is humanity itself."

(15) Zoe Druick, International Cultural Relations as a Factor in Postwar Canadian Cultural Policy: The Relevance of UNESCO for the Massey Commission, published by Simon Fraser University

(16) Karen Finlay, "The Force of Culture: Vincent Massey and Canadian Sovereignty", University of Toronto Press, 2004

(17) Anna Upchurch, Vincent Massey: Linking Cultural Policy from Great Britain to Canada, International Journal of Cultural Policy, Feb. 15, 2008

(18) This came to be known as the Order of Canada, instituted in 1967, and quickly followed by a succession of other Canadian honours in the years following. It is vital to understand that the origin of the honours' authority is derived directly from the British Monarchy, which is legally acknowledged as being the "Fount of All Honours". This is the fundamental source from which all efficient authority springs up within both the public and shadow governing functions of the British Imperial system.

(19) Preliminary Report Royal Commission on Canada's Economic Prospects, Toronto: Cockfield, Brown p. 83

(20) Stephen Azzi, Foreign Investment and the Paradox of Economic Nationalism, published in Canadas of the Mind: The Making and Unmaking of Canadian Nationalism in the 20th Century, McGill-Queens University Press, 2007

(21) While Finance Minister Gordon's measures to impose foreign takeover taxes of 30%, and incentives for Canadian ownership of the economy in order to cut off American capital flows into Canada, the devastating effects to the economy could not be ignored and they were soon disbanded. Many of Gordon's propositions such as the Canadian Development Corporation to pool capital and buy back Canada would only go into effect during the Trudeau administration 10 years later.

(22) One of those who suffered the purge was C.D. Howe-ally Henry Erskine Kidd, General Secretary for the Liberal Party who refered to the process led by Gordon as "a palace revolution", as referenced in Stephen Azzi, Walter Gordon and Rise of Canadian Nationalism, McGill-Queens University Press, 1999, pg. 71

(23) "I have a feeling that people would like to follow your star in droves – if and when you decide the time is right to give them the nod." Cited in Walter Gordon and the Rise of Canadian Nationalism by Stephen Azzi, p.70

(24) Glassco Commission Royal Commission Report on Government Organization, Queen's Printer, Ottawa Canada, 1962, vol. 3, part 1, p.22

(25) Ibid. p. 22

(26) Ibid., p.33

(27) Ibid., p.33

(28) During a confrontation with the Lamontagne Senate Committee, Secretary of the Treasury Board Simon Reisman described the problem of PPB thus: "PPB may, for all I know, have considerable merit when applied to business operations... the PPB system, however, in more complex situations such as science, breaks down by reason of the general error of its assumption that the outcome of experiments is predictable." [Excerpted from F.Roland Hayes' Chaining of Prometheus: The Evolution of a Power Structure for Canadian Science, University of Toronto Press, 1973, p.19]

(29) Robert Chodos, Let Us Prey, Jarmes Lorimer and Company publishing, 1974, p.26

(30) Lamontagne, a disciple both of Father Levesque at Laval University and Joseph Schumpeter at Harvard, collaborated with Walter Gordon as a member of the 1955 Royal Commission on Economic Prospects for Canada before going on to become personal secretary to Lester Pearson in 1958. Previous to his chairmanship of the Senate Committee, Lamontagne was President of the Privy Council Office (1964-65), before being made Senator by Lester B. Pearson.

(31) Maurice Lamontagne, Report of the Senate Special Committee on Science Policy, vol. 1, p.22

(32) Lyndon LaRouche, On the Subject of Oligarchy, Executive Intelligence Review, July 26, 2013

(33) ibid.

(34) Report of the Special Senate Committee on Science Policy, vol. 2, p.33-34

(35) Maurice Lamontagne, Report of the Senate Special Committee on Science Policy, vol. 1, p.240

(36) Lamontagne, 29 March 1969, Senate Debates, cited in F. Roland Hayes' The Chaining of Prometheus, pg.186

(37) Matthew Ehret-Kump, Diefenbaker and the Sabotage of the Northern Vision, The Canadian Patriot #4, Jan 2013

(38) Former Governor General Roland Michener, himself a Rhodes Scholar, also received the Royal Victorian chain by Queen Elizabeth II for services rendered to the British Empire. This honour is the highest given out by the Monarchy, of which only 14 have ever been distributed, and only two in Canada`s history. The other chain was given to Vincent Massey.

(39) The official formation of the Canadian Club of Rome took place only in 1974. Although Trudeau was an enthusiastic participant at Club of Rome meetings, even sponsoring the 1971 Conference in Montebello, Quebec which gave birth to the work "Limits to Growth" the following year, he did not become an officially registered member until out of office. Trudeau remained close friends with Alexander King, and according to former U.S. Ambassador Thomas Enders, Trudeau referred "frequently to Club of Rome thinking on the need for new political and moral approaches". Trudeau's renown as a Club of Rome representative was so great that after Aurelio Peccei's death in 1984, Rhodes Scholar J. Gordon King revealed that Trudeau was even asked to become Peccei's replacement... a post which he turned down due to political reasons at that time. [see The Limits to Influence: The Club of Rome and Canada 1968-1988 by Jason Churchill, Waterloo, Ontario, 2006, p.138.]

Appendix 1

Cecil Rhodes Calls for the Recapturing of America

In 1877, while laying out his agenda for the formation of a secret society to recapture Britain's lost colony of America and the submission of "inferior" races (ie. non anglo-saxon) under the control of a renewed British Empire, Cecil Rhodes, wrote his Confessions of Faith in which the following explicit mission statement can be read:

"I contend that we are the finest race in the world and that the more of the world we inhabit the better it is for the human race. Just fancy those parts that are at present inhabited by the most despicable specimens of human beings what an alteration there would be if they were brought under Anglo-Saxon influence, look again at the extra employment a new country added to our dominions gives. I contend that every acre added to our territory means in the future birth to some more of the English race who otherwise would not be brought into existence... I look into history and I read the story of the Jesuits I see what they were able to do in a bad cause and I might say under bad leaders.

Why should we not form a secret society with but one object the furtherance of the British Empire and the bringing of the whole uncivilised world under British rule for the recovery of the United States for the making the Anglo-Saxon race but one Empire...

We know the size of the world we know the total extent. Africa is still lying ready for us it is our duty to take it. It is our duty to seize every opportunity of acquiring more territory and we should keep this one idea steadily before our eyes that more territory simply means more of the Anglo-Saxon race more of the best the most human, most honourable race the world possesses. To forward such a scheme what a splendid help a secret society would be a society not openly acknowledged but who would work in secret for such an object."

Rhodes' agenda had manifested itself upon his death in 1902 with the creation of the Rhodes Scholarship Trust whose trustees included Lord Rothschild, and Lord Alfred Milner. The Canadian imperialist George Parkin had even left his post as headmaster of Upper Canada College in Toronto, in order to serve as the 1st head of the Scholarship Trust from 1902-1922. Both Parkin and Milner went on to mentor a young Vincent Massey.

Appendix 2:
Lyndon LaRouche Destroys Systems Analysis

"On the day on which, existing money goes out of existence, as in Weimar Germany 1923, but this time more or less world-wide, what do the existing accountants do?

If we are to recover from the social effects of the currently onrushing disintegration of the present world financial and monetary systems, radically new methods of cost accounting will be required for private enterprises, as also for governmental and related kinds of institutions. The previously used, linear, "connect the dots" tactics, of both financial accounting and of systems analysis, must be abandoned, and replaced. A new standard must be adopted, for cost-accounting, budgetary, tariff, taxation policies, national-income estimations, and related practices.

The pivotal question of all competent cost accounting, is: What causes an increase in the net physical value of the productive powers of labor? For a moment, put aside calculations made in terms of nominal, that is to say financial, prices. Think solely in terms of physical contents of market-baskets of goods and services; measure inputs, as costs (inputs), and as outputs, in those physical terms. Instead of the common practice, of simply comparing ratios of prices of nominal inputs and outputs, seek to define the processes which determine a succession of changes in ratios of physical outputs to physical inputs. As measured in those terms, which increases, or decreases, in specific qualities of expenditure for infrastructure, production and distribution of product, and of which kinds of products, have neither beneficial, nor detrimental impact upon the functionally determined rate of net physical output, as the latter may be measured per capita of both total labor-force and population, and per square kilometer of a nation's, or region's surface-area?

Competent answers to those questions, lie outside the domain of a cost accounting based upon financial analysis, and outside the tyranny of those recently popular, pseudo-scientific hoaxes known as the "systems analysis" of the late John von Neumann and the statistical "information theory" of the late Professor Norbert Wiener. In the circumstances defined by the present crisis, we can no longer tolerate those faulty practices, which have been generally accepted standards of professional and related practice for much too long."

Download the full article The Becoming Death of Systems Analysis published in the March 31, 2000 issue of Executive Intelligence review at www.larouchepub.com/lar/2000/lar_systems_analysis_2713.html

Also, see LaRouche's 1981 paper: Systems Analysis is White Collar Genocide also available on www.larouchepub.com

Manufactured by Amazon.ca
Bolton, ON

15421517R00039